T4-AJF-704

Emergency Planning and Management in College Libraries

CLIP Note # 17

Compiled by

Susan C. George
Physical Sciences Librarian
Dartmouth College
Hanover New Hampshire

College Library Information Packet Committee
College Libraries Section
Association of College and Research Libraries
A Division of the American Library Association

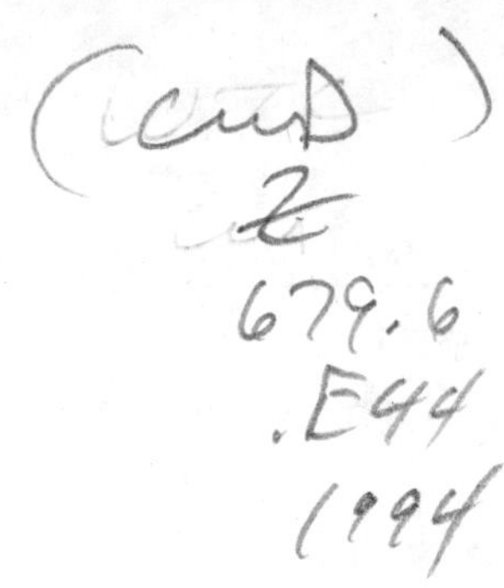

ASSOCIATION OF COLLEGE & RESEARCH LIBRARIES

Published by the Association of College and Research Libraries
A Division of the American Library Association
50 East Huron Street
Chicago, IL 60611-2795
1-800-545-2433

ISBN: 0-8389-7710-3

This publication is printed on recycled paper.

Printed in the United States of America.

TABLE OF CONTENTS

CLIP NOTES COMMITTEE

INTRODUCTION

Objective

The College Library Information Packet *Notes* publishing program under the auspices of the College Libraries Section of the Association of College and Research Libraries, provides "college and small university libraries with state-of-the-art reviews and current documentation on library practices and procedures of relevance to them." (Morein, 226) This *CLIP Note* offers information about emergency planning and management for libraries.

Background

Emergency planning and management is not a part of the library school curriculum, nor is it a task listed on a professional job description; yet, library emergencies (or disasters) do occur and too often, we are not prepared. The rationale for this document is three-fold:

•to survey the policies and procedures for emergency planning and management in college and small university libraries;

•to alert libraries to the many types of disasters which exist, any of which may befall them;

•to provide library staffs with useful tools to develop workable mechanisms for dealing with these events.

This CLIP Note was undertaken to assess how college libraries are dealing with the issues of emergency planning and management.

Survey Procedure

The *CLIP Notes* Committee of the College Libraries Section of ACRL reviewed the proposal and drafts of a questionnaire. In June 1992, 261 small and medium-sized academic libraries received the revised questionnaire. All of these libraries had previously agreed to participate in the *CLIP Notes* program and all serve institutions with enrollments between 1,000 and 5,000 students and are classified as "Comprehensive Universities and Colleges I" or "Liberal Arts Colleges I" in *A Classification of Institutions of Higher Education* (Carnegie Foundation for the Advancement of Teaching, 1987).

In addition to completing the questionnaire, those libraries with disaster-related documentation were asked to provide copies of any and/or all documentation which had been developed.

Survey Results

A total of 175 of the 261 questionnaires were returned for a 67% response rate. Apart from demographic and fiscal information specific to the responding institutions, each library was asked a series of questions regarding their preparedness for emergency management in their library.

General Information

Approximately two-thirds of the surveyed libraries have one central library for all subject areas. Almost one-half of the responding libraries are the sole occupant of their building; of the fifty-one percent who share occupancy, the majority have an academic department as the other tenant. The largest percentage of the libraries who share building space, occupy between 71-99% of the building. The location of the library within the shared space is not consistent: in the largest percentage, the library is 'above' all other occupants; almost an equal number state that the library and other occupants are a 'total mix'; and a significant number report that the library is 'central' to the building occupants.

Emergency Planning and Management

A slim majority of responding libraries (57%) have never experienced a disaster of any kind. Of the libraries who have experienced a disaster, one-half have a disaster manual and almost as many have a disaster team in place. The most frequently reported disaster is water, with mold/mildew reported one-half as many times. Disaster manuals are heavily oriented to fire and water problems. A large number include evacuation plans for staff and users, while fewer than one-half include a list of collection priorities.

While the majority of disaster teams are composed of people from all levels of staff (52%); a significant number of libraries (29%) have teams composed from the professional staff alone. Many team members are assigned or appointed (45%) and most teams report to the Library Director (84%). Most teams do not have a formal charge (77%) and do not meet regularly (71%). However, more than one-half of the team members have received training in emergency planning and management, mostly through workshops (32%). More than three-fourths of the responding libraries do not offer training courses to either librarians, support staff or student assistants.

Fewer than one-tenth of the responding libraries have a Risk Assessment Office; indeed, many responded that they did not understand the concept. Most libraries (41%) do not have a checklist of people within their own institution to contact when a disaster occurs and only fourteen percent have a checklist of on-campus emergency equipment available for use. Most libraries do not have a checklist of off-site disaster recovery suppliers and services (85%) and most do not have a checklist of outside consultants who specialize in managing specific types of disasters (82%).

Most libraries (better than 95%) have emergency equipment inspected regularly and one-half of the respondents have a policy that requires surge-protectors for computer terminals, photocopiers, etc. Ninety-four percent believe they have adequate signage regarding emergency exits; all who have adequate signage maintain that the signage is clearly visible. Many libraries (78%) indicate that emergency egress is available for the physically-challenged.

Most libraries (96%) do not have a written hazard analysis document. Most libraries (78%) do know the location of circuit breakers and do have access to them. Slightly more than one-half of the libraries (59%) do have access to insurance information and agree that the plan is periodically evaluated to insure that the coverage is adequate.

Almost one-half (46%) of the libraries maintain a collection of books and journal articles on disasters and their management, but fewer than one-half of their institutions (39%) require a formal report about the occurrence of a disaster.

In terms of security, most libraries use some type of detection system (3M, Checkpoint, etc.); one library, however, indicates that 'inexpensive photocopying' deters theft. It is also obvious from the responses, that many libraries use a combination of methods.

It is obvious from the responses to this survey, that most libraries do not consider themselves adequately prepared to deal with an emergency of any nature. Comments range from "we'll know more after our first disaster" to "pray hard!" clearly indicate that being prepared is not considered a priority task. On the other hand, those libraries who do have a Disaster Manual/Team, even if only 'in progress', seem to better understand the results of being unprepared.

Selection of Documents

In response to the survey, 19 libraries sent copies of their Disaster Manuals, a number of them prepared in electronic format. In addition, 3 libraries sent tables of contents, 1 library sent a copy of its emergency procedures, 1 library sent a draft copy of its disaster manual, and 1 library sent a copy of their statewide disaster plan. While all Manuals could not be reproduced because of space considerations, 6 are included to demonstrate the variety of ways in which libraries prepare for and manage emergencies of all types.

Bibliography

Allen, Susan M. (1990). Theft in Libraries or Archives. *College and Research Libraries News*, 51, 939-943.

Berdie, Douglas R., John F. Anderson and Marsha A. Niebuhr. (1986). *Questionnaires: Design and Use*. 2d. ed. Metuchen, NJ: Scarecrow Press.

Buchanan, Sally. (1980). Disaster Prevention and Action. *Oklahoma Librarian*, 30, 35-41.

Buchanan, Sally. (1981). Disaster: Prevention, Preparedness and Action. *Library Trends*, 30, 241-252.

Carnegie Council on Policy Studies in Higher Education. (1987). *A Classification of Higher Education*, rev. ed. Berkeley, California: The Carnegie Foundation for the Advancement of Teaching.

Davis, Mary B., Susan Fraser and Judith Reed. (1991). Preparing for Library Emergencies: A Cooperative Approach. *Wilson Library Bulletin, 66*, 42-44.

George, Susan C. and Cheryl T. Naslund. (1986). Library Disasters: A Learning Experience. *College and Research Libraries News, 47*, 251-257

Gunter, Linda. (1990). Earthquake Recovery at the Libraries of the Claremont Colleges. *College and Research Libraries News, 51*, 935-936.

Johnson, Linda B. and Jeff Paul. (1990). Coping with a Quake. *College and Research Libraries News*, 51, 928-933.

Macklin, Lisa A. and Martha K. Tarlton. (1991). Emergency Management and Disaster Mitigation Periodicals: An Annotated Bibliography. *Serials Review*, 17, 21-26.

Morein, P. Grady. (1985). What is a CLIP Note? *College and Research Libraries News*, 46, 226-229.

Naslund, Cheryl T. and Susan C. George. (1986). Insurance Settlement Negotiation. *College and Research Libraries News*, 47, 325-328.

Waters, Peter. (1975). *Procedures for Salvage of Water Damaged Library Materials*. Washington: Library of Congress.

SURVEY RESULTS

General Information

1. Number of FTE students enrolled:
   480 - 6324, average = 1,810

2. Number of FTE librarians:
   2 - 18.5, average = 5.86

3. Number of FTE support staff:
   1.5 - 37, average = 7.96

4. Number of FTE student assistants:
   0 - 59, average = 11.5

5. Number of physical volumes in all libraries on campus (at end of fiscal year, June 30, 1992): *34,000 - 1,600,000, average = 234,432*

6. Library location(s) on campus:

   129 one central library for all subject areas
   46 one central library and branch libraries

   How many branches?
   16 libraries , 1 branch
   14 libraries , 2 branches
   10 libraries ,3 branches
   4 libraries ,4 branches
   1 library , 7 branches
   1 library ,5 branches

7. Library buildings on campus: Is the library the only occupant of its building? *yes 86, no 89*

   a. who are the other occupants?(please specify)

   32 academic depts
   10 academic depts/classrooms
   10 labs
   5 competence center
   4 computer services
   2 administration/storage
   2 classrooms/archives
   2 not answered
   2 offices
   2 offices/snack bar
   1 academic dept/commercial
   1 archives/foundation
   1 business school

b. what percent of the building space does the library occupy?

0-10% = 6 *11-20% = 3*
21-30% = 2 *31-40% = 4*
41-50% = 3 *51-60% = 3*
61-70% = 6 *71-80% = 20*
81-90% = 22 *91-100% =20*

c. where is the library located in relation to the other occupants of the building?

27 library is above *23 total mix of occupants*
12 library is central *9 not answered*
8 library is adjacent *4 library surrounds*
3 library is below *1 library is south*
1totally separate *1 library is surrounded by*

Emergency Planning and Management

1. Have any of your libraries experienced a disaster? *yes 75, no 100*

If **yes**, which of the following types apply (*check all that apply*):

64 water *33 mold/mildew 3*
16 theft *11 mutilation/vandalism*
7 fire *6 natural disaster (earthquake, etc.)*
4 pets *other: 1 asbestos*

2. Does your library have a disaster manual? *Please return a copy of your manual with the survey questionnaire. (Not all manuals will be included in their entirety)* *yes 36, no 139*

If yes

a. how often is the manual revised?

15 annual *5 as needed*
2 not answered *2 every 2 years*
2 no schedule *2 every 5 years*
2 not yet *2 not answered*
1 every 3 yrs *1 when staff changes*
1 first edition *1 annual for telephone list, remainder revised every 5 yrs*

b. who is responsible for the revision?

8 Library Director	*4 not answered*
4 Preservation	*4 Disaster Team*
*2 A librarian**	*2 Committee**
*1 Reference librarian **	*1 professional staff*
1 Safety	*1 Archivist/Library Director*
1 Head, Technical Services	*1 Disaster Plan Coordinator*
1 Business Manager/Librarian	
1 Associate Director	*1 Security*
1 Special Collections Librarian	
1 Librarian/staff/security	*1 Serials Librarian/Preservation Administrator*

unspecified

c. to whom is the manual distributed?

6 all staff	*5 anyone/everyone*
5 library staff +security	*2 professionals/Provost/safety/B&G*
4 Service points/B&G	*1 all building supervisors*
1 not answered	*1 need to know*
1 all dept heads	*1 Archivist/Registrar*
1 Maintenance	*1 Security/Library Director*
1 staff/security/Preservation	*1 Disaster Team/Circ desks 1*
1 all staff/local fire dept/safety/Business Office	

d. is the manual an 'umbrella' document (for the entire library system), not specific to each to each library unit? *yes 27, no 7, not answered 2*

if **no**, are there specific plans for each library unit?
yes 1, no 4, not answered 2

e. what types of disasters are documented in the manual? *(e.g. fire, water, earthquake, etc).*

27 fire	*20 water*
4 bomb threat	*4 earthquake*
4 power failure	*3 vandalism*
3 weather	*3 medical*
2 pests	*2 all problems*
2 natural disasters	*1 accident*
1 disruptive patron	*1 not answered*
1 theft	*1 computer damage*
1 predictable events (hurricanes)	

f. does the manual include an evacuation plan for staff and users? *yes 27, no 6, not answered 3*

If **yes**, do you rehearse the plan? *yes 13, no 14*

If **yes**, how often?

7 annual	*2 semiannual*
2 not answered	*1 undecided*
1 every 2-3 yrs	

g. does the manual include procedures for dealing with automated systems and their recovery?

yes 8, no 23, not answered 4, none in building 1

h. does the manual include a list of collection priorities (i.e., what collections or areas of the library should receive attention first, second, etc.)? *yes 14, no 17, not answered 5*

3. Does your library have a Disaster Team? *yes 31, no 143, not answered 1*

If yes

a. how many members are on the team?

7 libraries have 5 members | *6 libraries have 4 members*
4 libraries have 6 members | *3 libraries have 7 members*
3 libraries have 2 members | *2 libraries have 12 members*
2 libraries have 11 members | *2 libraries have 9 members*
2 libraries have 3 members

of the 31 respondents, the average number of team members is 5.8

b. what is the composition of the team?*(i.e., from what departments are members selected? are librarians and support staff selected?)*

9 professional staff | *16 all staff*
1 not answered | *1 Director+dept heads*
1 Preservation Committee | *1 Collection Management Librarian+staff*
1 librarian+security+physical plant
1 Special Collections librarian+Conservation librarian

c. how are the members selected?

4 not answered | *14 assigned/appointed*
3 personal interest | *3 knowledge/need*
2 volunteer | *2 by function*
2 concensus | *1 area of responsibility*

d. to whom, in the library, does the team report?

26 Library Director | *2 Associate Director*
1 not answered | *1 Preservation Head*
1 Serials Librarian/Preservation Administrator

e. does the team meet regularly? *yes 8, no 22, not answered 1*

f. does the team have a formal charge?*(Please return a copy of the charge with the survey questionnaire)* *yes 6, no 24, not answered 1*

g. has the team received training in emergency planning and management? *yes 19, no 11, not answered 1*

If **yes**, how is the team trained?

1 not answered | *10 workshops*
1 attend state meetings | *1 video*
1 local emergency agencies+literature
1 drills, videos, workshops | *1 workshops, tapes, courses*
1 twice in 5 yrs | *1 by Associate Director/Conservation Director 1*
1 by college and others (not specified)

4. Are training courses offered to:

librarians?	*yes 34, no 124, not answered 16*
support staff?	*yes 33, no 125, not answered 16*
student assistants?	*yes 18, no 134, not answered 22*
other	*not applicable 1*

***NOTE**: one NO response indicated that 'liability' was the reason for not providing courses.*

If **yes**, please indicate the course types offered (e.g., CPR, first-aid, use of fire extinguishers, fire drill, etc.):

12 fire extinguishers	*4 fire drills/safety*
8 fire drills	*3 CPR*
2 CPR/first aid	*2 not answered*
2 CPR/first aid/fire extinguishers	
1 proper lifting	*1 first aid*
1 stress release	*1 safety*
1 all emergency procedures	*1 recovery techniques*
1 video	*1 CPR/fire drills*
1 CPR/Fire extinguishers	*1 fire drills/first aid*
1 fire drills/fire extinguishers/water recovery	
1 evaluation/protection/repair	
1 CRP/fire drills/earthquake drills	

How often are courses offered?

11 annual	*7 as needed/requested*
6 not answered	*2 every 2 years*
2 semiannual	*2 every 2-3 years*
1 regular	*1 each term*

Who sponsors/schedules the offered courses?(e.g. library, other campus department?)

13 library	*5 not answered*
3 safety	*2 consortium*
2 library/physical plant	
1 Personnel	*1 Fire marshal*
1 security	*1 Library Staff Development committee*
1university	*1 health center*
1 outside	*1 campus facilities*

5. Does your institution have a Risk Assessment Office?

yes 6, no 159, not answered 9, do not know 1

If **yes**, please describe the mission of that Office (*or attach a a copy of their mission statement to the survey questionnaire*).

3 mission not described	*1 no mission*
1 not applicable	*1 for insurance purposes*

***mission**: the Assistant to the VP for Administration also serves as Safety Officer reviewing insurance and health policies, etc. We also have a hazardous materials officer.*

Please also describe your use of their services.

4 not answered *1 review of manual*
1 inventory of materials to store off-site

6. Does your library have a checklist of people <u>within your institution</u> to contact when a disaster occurs? *yes 72, no 100, not answered 2*

If yes

a. how is the list arranged?

10 not answered	*8 type of disaster*
8 function	*6 priority*
7 telephone tree	*3 by department*
3 areas	*2 hierarchial*
2 not applicable	*1 alphabetical*
1 library security	*1 not written*
1 who to call 1	*1 chain of command*
1 proximity to College	*1 categories*
1 through Physical Plant Director	
1 Emergency Coordinator/Conservation Coordinator	

b. does it include people from outside the library who have expertise in emergency management? *yes 38, no 29, not answered 5*

c. is the checklist updated regularly? *yes 38, no 21, not answered 12, not applicable 1*

how often?

18 annual	*6 not answered*
4 biannual	*5 as needed*
3 semiannual	*1 every few yrs*
1 varies	

7. Does your library have a checklist of on-campus emergency equipment (freezer space, fans, wet vacs, etc.) available for use? *yes 25, no 149, maybe 1*

If yes

a. is the checklist updated regularly? *yes 14, no 7, not answered 4*

how often?

8 annual	*2 not answered*
2 biannual	*1 monthly*

b. is the checklist in a location accessible to all?

yes 12, no 3, not answered 10

8. Does your library have a checklist of off-site disaster recovery suppliers and services? *(if **yes**, please include a copy with your survey questionnaire)*

yes 24, no 149, not answered 2

If yes

a. is the checklist updated regularly? *yes 12, no 11, not answered 1*

how often?

7 annual	*2 not set*
2 not answered 2	*1 biannual*

b. is the checklist in a location accessible to all?

yes 13, no 9, not answered 2

9. Does your library have a checklist of outside consultants who specialize in managing specific types of disasters? *(if **yes**, please include a copy of the list with your survey questionnaire)* *yes 28, no 144, not answered 3*

10. Is emergency equipment (*e.g., fire extinguishers*) within the library regularly inspected? *yes 167, no 6, not answered 2*

If **yes**, who inspects the equipment?

59 B&G	*42 Fire marshall/fire dept*
21 outside contract	*15 not answered*
13 safety	*10 security*
7 local government	*2 suppliers*
1 insurance company	*1 library staff*
1 fire extinguisher company	*1 name of an individual*

11. Does your library have a policy that requires surge-protectors for computer terminals, photocopiers, etc? *yes 86, no 86, not answered 3*

***NOTE**: of the no responses, 11 stated that protectors are 'practice, but not policy'.*

If **yes**, is the policy enforced? *yes 83, no 2, not answered 1*

12. Does your library have adequate signage regarding emergency exits?

yes 165, no 10

If yes,

Is the signage clearly visible? *yes 166, no 6, not answered 3*

Is emergency egress available for the physically-challenged? *yes 129, no 41, not answered 5*

***NOTE**: of the YES responses, 11 indicated limited egress because of elevators being disabled during an emergency.*

13. Is there a written hazard analysis (i.e., protection from predictable losses) document available for each library on campus?

yes 8, no 161, not answered 4, do not know 2

14. Is the location of circuit breakers for the library known to you and/or others on the Disaster Team? *yes 137, no 33, not answered 4, some 1*

Do you and/or others on the Disaster Team have access to the breakers? *yes 123, no 6, not answered 8*

15. Is institutional insurance coverage information available to you? *yes 104, no 64, not answered 5, do not know 2*

Is this plan periodically assessed to determine that the coverage is adequate? *yes 77, no 13, not answered 7, do not know 6, not yet 1*

If **yes**, by whom is the plan reviewed?

9 not answered	*7 Business Office*
7 Financial Office	*7 VP Business*
6 Library Director/Financial Office	
5 VP Finance	*5 VP**
3 Treasurer	*3 Library Director/Business Office*
3 VP Business/Library Director	
2 Library Director	*2 Purchasing/Library Director*
2 VP Administration	*2 Purchasing Agent*
2 Insurance company	*2 Administration*
1 do not know	*1 B&G/Treasurer*
1 safety	*1 outside consultant*
1 Dean of Administration	*1 Asst Controller*
1 Librarian/VP Finance	*1 Risk Management/Dean*
1 Physical Plant Director	*1 College Librarian/Special Librarian*
1 Library Director/Insurance Coordinator	

**unspecified*

If **yes**, how often is the plan reviewed?

25 annual	*23 not answered*
9 not known	*7 every 2 years*
4 every few years	*2 not scheduled*
1 not applicable	*1 biannual*
1 every 3 years	*1 unsure*
1 irregular	*1 every 5 years*

16. Does your library maintain a collection of books and journal articles on disasters and their management? *yes 82, no 92, not answered 1*

17. Does your library/institution require that reports be filled out on disasters sustained? *yes 61, no 91, not answered 7, not known 13, not needed to date 1, never had one 1, probably 1*

If **yes**, to whom are the reports routed?

13 Business Office
8 Physical plant
6 not answered
5 Security
5 Library Director
4 Finance
4 Provost
*3 Dean**
*2 Senior VP**
2 Provost/VP Physical Plant
2 do not know
*2 Administration**
1 Library Director/Provost
1 involved campus departments
1 Director Campus Facilities
1 Preservation/VP Academic Affairs
1 Academic Dean/Physical Plant Director
1 depends on disaster
1 Dean of Faculty/Police Dept
1 Library Director/VP Administration & Business
1 Serials Librarian/Preservation Officer

**unspecified*

18. How does your library discourage/prevent theft? (e.g., security detectors, etc.)

138 3M system
9 checkpoint system
5 yes
4 honor system
4 alarms on doors
4 alarms on irregular exits
4 not answered
4 single entrance/exit
4 monitors/TV screens/cameras
4 campus security
3 exit check (by guard)
3 screens on windows/fixed windows
2 training students
2 student newspaper
2 complex door locks
2 closed stacks/limited access
2 routine police visits
1 inexpensive photocopying
1 ineffective
1 target system
1 Lucasey VCR plates
1 students at front desk
1 night lights
1 security+honor system
1 staff vigilence
1 display of damaged items
1 lockdowns on computer equipment
1 motion/heat detectors in archives

19. How do you assess your institution's ability to deal with a library disaster?

24 poor
12 low priority
8 not very well
5 good
4 good/very good
2 moderate
2 below average
19 not answered
9 adequate/average
6 not adequate
5 reasonably well
2 very bad
2 do not know
2 use crisis management
16 fair
8 not well prepared
6 good position
5 fairly well organized
2 depends on disaster
2 close to minimal
2 moderate disaster OK, large one no
2 we'll know more after our first disaster
1 pray hard!
1 probably able...
1 slow
1 deficient
1 no plan
1 lousy
1 B+->A
1 abominable
1 not very high
1 'F'
1 C-
1 growing
1 very limited
1 practically nil
1 no idea
1 barely adequate
1 improving
1 not close
1 well equipped
1 phone
1 look at plan
1 unprepared
1 mediocre at best
1 laughable
1 need to address issue
1 as good as any library
1 great spirit of teamwork
1 not very professional
1 disaster-a poor plan
1 '7' for earthquakes
1 OK on an ad-hoc basis
1 contact Business Manager/Physical Plant
1 excellent, once training is completed
1 limited - plans and documents lacking
1 too much common knowledge/not enough documentation

LIBRARY DISASTER PLANS

Emerson College Library Disaster Plan

SPECIFIC PROCEDURES

SALVAGE AFTER WATER DISASTERS

The complete restoration of bound, water soaked documents can be costly. In the majority of cases, costs do not justify salvage and restoration of books in print or replaceable items. Replacement is nearly always much less costly than restoration.

Freeze drying is the most effective method for removing water from large numbers of books and paper artifacts, but it isn't the final step. After drying, restoration and rebinding are necessary. These add to costs.

When it is hot and humid, salvage must be initiated without delay in order to prevent mold growth. 48 hours is all it takes for mold to begin appearing in an unventilated area. Most damage to bound volumes occurs within the first 8 hours of the soaking.

1. Put plastic sheeting over stack ranges in affected areas to eliminate further damage. Cover all work surfaces with polyethylene sheeting and empty all unnecessary equipment and furnitue from packing and drying areas.
2. Call in experts for advice and notify insurance company.
3. Remove wet books from stacks and place in the drying room.

PRELIMINARIES TO REMOVAL FROM AFFECTED AREAS

A. Human chains should be used to remove materials from each shelf and pack them in marked crates. (See Removal and Packing)
B. Fungicidal fogging may be necessary if mold is found. This should be done only under the supervision of a competent chemist of conservator.
C. Ship packed materials to freezers within a few hours.

REMOVAL AND PACKING

These steps require two equally staffed teams of people. One team will pass materials from the affected areas and the other will pack them.

General instructions include:

Do NOT open wet books, separate single sheets, remove covers of water soaked materials, disturb wet file boxes, prints, drawings or photographs. Volumes found in the aisles will be most damaged. Rapid swelling caused them to burst from shelves and now, in addition, they have sustained the shock of falling and immersion. Submerged shelves usually have a mix of wet and partially wet volumes. The wet ones can be identified because they are misshapen and by their concave spines and convex fore-edges. These will need to be rebound after drying.

1. Remove sodden materials from aisles in exact condition in which they were found
2. Pack wettest material first.
3. Remove very damp and partially wet materials next.
4. Remove dry materials to controlled environment with air spaces between them.
5. Sterilize and return shelves, walls, floors and ceilings to normal conditions. Sterilization is important and requires changing scrub water often, use of fresh mops

and rags, cleaning corners and under bottom shelves of stacks

6. Heat can be used for drying if good air circulation and dehumidification can be established.
7. Install hygothermographs to record temperature and relative humidity.
8. Moisture-content meters are useful for measuring the moisture in the materials themselves.

CLEANING AND DRYING WITHOUT FREEZING

NOTE: All books printed on coated stock must be frozen while wet and vacuum dried.

1. Set up drying rooms well away from affected area.
2. Drying rooms need controlled environment which will remove moisture-laden air and which can be maintained at a constant temperature.
3. Maintain cleanliness by prompt removal of wet debris.
4. Assign task of keeping floors and work areas as clean as possible to one or more persons.
5. Separate wet materials into small units by loose packaging or individual wrapping. This permits free flow of air around them and prevents the crushing which occurs when materials collect in large piles.
6. Wash mud deposits off books in clean running water. Hold one closed book at a time under water and use gentle, dabbing action with sponge to remove mud. (NOTE: There are several types of books which should not be washed under any circumstances. The advice of a conservator would be helpful in making these decisions.)
7. If material is exposed to mud-saturated water, freezing is a good option. Books can be treated after freezing. The best time to remove silt is before drying, but this is best done off-site.

CONVENTIONAL DRYING OF WET BOOKS WITH COVERS INTACT

1. After washing, stand books upright on several sheets of absorbent paper. Books should be on head end with covers open slightly. Let stand while draining, replacing absorbent paper frequently.
2. Place thymol-impregnated sheets between front and back covers and flyleaves. To prepare sheets, cut unprinted newsprint into sheets of graduated sizes according to size of books to be treated.4X6 inches, 5X7 inches, 8X10 inches and 10X12 inches are usually adequate. Working outdoors with gloves, goggles and masks, dip each sheet in a 10-15% solution of thymol chrystals in ethanol, acetone, industrial denatured alcohol or trichlorethane (1 pound/gallon of solvent). Air dry sheets on polyethylene-covered tables. Bundle and wrap in aluminum foil or polyethylene and store in a cool place.
3. Place aluminum foil, polyester, or polyethylene film between hymol-impregnated paper and leaves of book.

INTERLEAVING

1. On first attempt do not open covers of book to more than a 30 degree angle. As soon as safe, interleave with sheets of treated newsprint or paper towels at every

50 pages. Start from the back of the book. Keep upright during first stage of interleaving.

2. Don't interleave too much. Spine should not be concave or volume distorted.
3. Change interleaving frequently.

DRYING DISTORTED BOOKS ON LINES

Hanging a partially dry volume on three or more short lines will help spine return to original shape as it dries. Lines should be of monofilament nylon, not more than one thirty-second of an inch in diameter, not more than 6 feet long and strung approximately 1/2 inch apart. Three lines will support volumes 1-1 1/2 inches thick. (DO NOT

HANG BOOKS WEIGHING MORE THAN 6 POUNDS.) Volumes are safe to hang if:

1. there is no water dripping from them.
2. they feel damp, not wet.
3. they can be opened easily throughout.

DRYING BOOKS WITH ONLY WET EDGES

1. Interleave with thymol-impregnated sheets.
2. Lay sheets of thymol-impregnated paper over sheets of clean blotting paper and place these inside the front and back boards.
3. Shut the book and place it on several sheets of absorbent paper.
4. As the drying process proceeds, the interleaving sheets can be removed to expose dry sections.
5. Turn item over after each interleaving.
6. When leaves are almost dry, place a light weight on the book.

NOTE: Books with only slightly wet edges can be placed on head ends and fanned open slightly in path of flow of heated air *or* hung to dry. To keep distortion to a minimum, lay volumes flat under light pressure just before drying is complete.

FINAL STAGE OF DRYING

1. When nearly dry, close books and lay them flat on horizontal surface.
2. Gently form them into normal shape.
3. Hold in place with a weight.

DO NOT STACK ON TOP OF EACH OTHER.

PREPARATION FOR FREEZING

1. Wash away accumulated mud and filth. (Do this if there are enough trained persons and time taken doesn't delay freezing the bulk of the material.)
2. Wrap bound volumes in freezer paper, wax paper, or silicone paper to prevent the items from sticking together. If damaged materials are to be vacuum or freeze dried packing them in milk crates can be substituted for wrapping.
3. Move wet items from library to freezer in refrigerated trucks. Dry ice and unrefrigerated trucks can be used when there are a small number of items. Use gloves when handling dry ice.

FREEZE DRYING

After materials are frozen it must be decided how they will be dried. The least expen sive and most succesful method is freeze drying. Evaluate materials to be restored in terms of amount of restoration and costs.

a. If moldy at time of freezing, items need sterilization. This is easily done with CO_2 or Freon at the end of vacuum drying.

b. Fog chamber with a solution of 12% thymol in trichlorethylene which increases resistance to further attacks.

If all water damaged materials aren't sterilized, which is recommended, follow these precautions:

1. Place all dried materials on open shelving in ventilated and air conditioned "rehabilitation" area, well separated from the main collections.
2. After 6 months of 35-45% relative humidity and temperature less than 65 degrees Farenheit, adjust the conditions to duplicate stack conditions.
3. For six more months, conduct daily spot checks for mold.
4. If there are no problems, return material to stacks. It is suggested hat a qualified conservator inspect materials before reshelving. Continue to check for mold for one year.

HANDLING SEPARATE SHEETS AND LEAVES

These materials are usually handled by freezing them and leaving the restoration to experts. In general:

1. Don't sponge.
2. Loose, single-sheets with no soluble components can be rinsed in running water.
3. Containers and contents should be frozen as found.

HANDLING WET MICROFILM

1. Once wet, keep silver halide film immersed in clean cool water in a plastic container until treatment is possible. It can remain wet for several days.
2. Diazo or vesicular film can be dried with a soft, lint-free cloth.

NOTE: Heat from fire may cause fading. 120-140 degrees Farenheit begins fading process. It is suggested that films not be stored in fire-resistant safes or cabinets with insulation. These, when heated, release moisture causing steam build up. This can melt the film.

EVALUATION OF LOSS

If covered by insurance, full settlement of a claim requires:

1. Listing of lost and damaged materials
2. Establishment of value of lost and damaged material
3. Determination of extent and success of possible restoration

It is suggested if a claim is anticipated, that every item is salvaged, frozen and dried.

POST-DISASTER ASSESSMENT

1. Hold a post-mortem meeting to determine what went right and wrong.
2. Write a report on the disaster.
3. Review and update disaster plan.
4. Evaluate supply and facility sources.
5. Send letters of thanks to all who helped.

York College Emergency Procedure Manual

VI. PROVISIONS FOR HANDICAPPED

A. Given the accessibility of all floors and areas to the non-ambulatory handicapped patron, the possibility exists that such persons could be in any part of the Library. This increases our concerns for the safety of those persons who may have entered the second floor from the elevator unnoticed by Library personnel and who may require assistance in making an emergency exit.

1. The second floor emergency exits at the southeast and southwest corners, as well as the main stairways, would be utilized to evacuate patrons since the nature of the emergency may render the elevator inoperable. Given the physical limitations, the size of the person, and availability of help, best judgment should be exercised in deciding the best possible route. In the event that time does not permit reaching a workable solution, patron should be placed at the safest exit and Library personnel should return to the main door to direct emergency assistance to the location of the person.
2. Elevator should be checked to ascertain that no one is trapped inside and apprise emergency personnel of the situation when they arrive. In the event of fire, do not, under any circumstances, use the elevator.
3. On routine food and noise patrols, Library personnel should make a mental note if a handicapped person is present.
4. Should circumstances allow for the removal of a handicapped person, place person in a safe location outside until further help arrives to handle the situation.
5. Periodicals and Audio Visual Services are equipped with ramped exits. In an emergency the Periodicals exit is the first choice for evacuating handicapped patrons, should time and situation permit. This exit is identified with the international symbol for wheelchair accessibility on the Library Floor Plans, Appendix A to this manual.

6. Should the Periodicals exit be inaccessible, the alternative handicapped evacuation exit is the Audio Visual Services Hallway.
   a. Access to this exit requires a key to the door at the end of the faculty office corridor.
   b. This key is clearly identified and is kept in the money drawer at the AV Services desk.

7. Should both Lower Level exits which are wheelchair accessible prove to be inappropriate for evacuation of the handicapped, Library personnel may have to physically carry the non-ambulatory patron to safety.

8. Given the wide variance possible in physical size, physical strength, and mobility between Library staff and the potential handicapped patron, evacuation of the non-ambulatory will no doubt call for best possible judgment on the part of Library staff.

DACUS LIBRARY EMERGENCY MANUAL

Winthrop College
Rock Hill, SC 29733
Revised September 30, 1986
October 22, 1990
August 26, 1991

INTRODUCTION

This manual is designed as a guide to action in event of crisis or emergency. All library staff should be familiar with its contents **BEFORE** an emergency occurs. A copy should be kept in an easily accessible location in each department.

All reporting procedures in this manual involve the use of the telephone. In the event of telephone failure, a reliable messenger should be sent to the appropriate office.

The procedures contained in this manual are for emergency use only. Non-emergency reports of equipment or building problems should be reported to the Dean's Administrative Specialist.

Winthrop College
Disaster Manual
This manual was based on a similar manual prepared for the Cornell University Libraries and the Basic Guidelines for Disaster Planning in Oklahoma.

TABLE OF CONTENTS

ANIMAL BITES

IMMEDIATE ACTION

A. **Rabies Danger**--Try to prevent repeated attack.

There may be danger of rabies. Try to prevent other people from being bitten. Rabid animals may be either hyperactive or may display some signs of paralysis.

B. **Call Public Safety Office**--Give the following information:

1. Description of the incident including description of the animal and its behavior.
2. Exact location (state "Library", floor, room).
3. Name of person who was bitten.
4. Your name.
5. Obtain name of animal's owner if possible.

C. **Contain Animal**--If safe to do so.

If possible have the animal isolated. This could simply mean evacuating a room and closing a door.

D. **Animal Removal Service Available**

The Public Safety Office upon request will send someone to remove animals. Library employees may, at their own risk, remove from a building animals which have not bitten a person. However, if the animal appears even slightly vicious or diseased, call Public Safety Office for assistance. **Do not attempt to remove an animal which appears dangerous.**

BOMB THREATS

IMMEDIATE ACTION

A. **Get Maximum Information**

Keep caller on the telephone if possible, and **WRITE DOWN** as much of the following information as you can obtain:

1. Exact location (state "Library", floor, room).
2. What time will the bomb go off?
3. What kind of bomb is it?
4. In what part of the building is it likely to be?
5. Any other information which might prove useful in determining location of bomb or identity of caller.

B. **Contact Switchboard**

1. Pull the fire alarm **only** if explosion appears imminent. The emergency plan used for clearing the building for fires may be used in clearing the building in a bomb threat situation. In addition to the standard procedure, have people **move away** from the building.
2. Report the bomb threat **IMMEDIATELY**. If the telephone is inoperative, report the threat to the switchboard in Tillman in person.

It is important that the Public Safety Office know immediately that this is a bomb threat rather than a fire. Your written notes will help them to determine what additional measures should be taken. Report the following:

a. The fire alarm signal at Dacus Library is actually a bomb threat.

b. Describe threat in detail, especially claimed **time** of explosion.
c. Give your name.
d. Meet the Emergency Area Coordinator or Public Safety officers at the main entrance, once more identifying yourself.

C. **Searching for Bomb**

Guidelines for Searching and Clearing Threat Areas:

Areas of Responsibility:

Public Safety Office and Maintenance Personnel will search the outside areas of the affected building, public areas, utility rooms, roof, utility tunnels, stairwells and elevators.

All personnel of the concerned building will be responsible for the search of offices, classrooms, laboratories, storage rooms, work areas, and corridors.

Supervisory personnel, in addition to supervising the internal search of the threatened building, will assist in searching of rooms not in use.

Priorities of the Search:

Upon direction by the Emergency Area Coordinator, the search of occupied buildings will commence simultaneously throughout the affected activity.

In unoccupied buildings, the search will be conducted by Maintenance and Public Service Personnel.

Action by the Search Party:

The search party will look for any unexplained or suspicious object which might contain an explosive device.

Examples:

1. Packages, suitcases, etc. found in toilets, stairways, trash containers, corridors, and elevators.
2. Unexplained objects left in office or work areas.
3. Vehicles, including trailers, vans, trucks, parked close to the threatened activity.
4. Any object that appears totally out of place.

The above are but a few examples. When there is any doubt about a suspicious object, it should be reported as a possible explosive device.

The Explosive Device:

If a suspected explosive device is discovered, its location will be reported to the Emergency Area Coordinator. **The search team will not disturb the suspected device unless so directed by the Emergency Area Coordinator.**

The area near the suspected device will be evacuated on order of the Emergency Action Coordinator who will then direct the reentering of the area.

D. **Notify Library Administration**

Call the Winthrop College Library Administration at you first opportunity. If there is no answer, call the Dean of Library Services or the Associate Dean of Library Services at home.

E. **Complete Bomb Threat Report Form**

A copy of this form follows this section.

F. **Await Further Orders from the Emergency Area Coordinator.**

WINTHROP COLLEGE
BOMB THREAT REPORT

Date_______________________

BUILDING TAKEOVER

IMMEDIATE ACTION

A. **KEEP CALM**

You help no one by panic and you may panic others.

B. **Do Not Defend the Library**

It is not your responsibility to act as a police officer. Resistance may only increase the destruction and bring about bodily harm to staff and patrons. It may also increase destruction of library materials.

C. **Notify the President of the College**

If he/she cannot be reached, notify the following in the order listed:

Assistant to the President
Vice-President for Academic Affairs
Public Safety Office
Vice-President for Business and Finance

This should be done whether the takeover is an actuality or simply appears to be possible. Give him/her the following information:

1. Exact Location (state "Library").
2. Describe the circumstances as clearly as possible.
   a. Where are the people?
   b. Is damage being done?
   c. Is the building occupied?
   d. Does the crowd seem rational and organized?
   e. How many people are there?
   f. Is there an obvious objective?
3. Give your name.

D. **Notify the Library Administration**

Also call the College Library Administration giving the exact information. The responsibility for decisions from that point will rest with the Administration and the Public Safety Office. If there is no answer in Adminis-tration--call the Dean of Library Services or the Associate Dean of Library Services at home.

E. **Talk**

If there appears to be a rational leader, a supervisor should talk to him/her in order to learn the purpose(s) of the takeover and any other relevant information. However, if it is a mob, acting irrationally, your first responsibil ity is for you own life and safety; your second responsibility is for the lives and safety of others in the building.

F. **Evacuate the Building**--by Asking People to Leave.

Use reasonable procedures to evacuate the building if there appears to be any danger to any individual. A discussion with the leader of the takeover may prove useful in effecting a peaceful, orderly evacuation.

G. **Follow Instruction given by Public Safety Office**.

CRIMINAL ACTIVITIES

IMMEDIATE ACTION

A. **Stay Calm**

Reassure victim of the crime.

B. **Obtain as much information as possible.**

Find out:

1. Nature of crime (theft, sexual assault, physical assault, disturbing the peace, etc.).
2. Location of crime (floor, exact area of library).
3. Description of suspect (hair color, height, race, sex, features, clothing, etc.).
4. Current location of suspect.

C. **Call the Public Safety Office**

Tell them:

1. "I want to report a crime in the library."
2. Your name and position.
3. Type of offense.
4. Description of suspect.
5. Action you think should be taken (send officer to library immediately, look for suspect in a certain area, etc.).

DRUG AND PSYCHIATRIC EMERGENCIES

IMMEDIATE ACTION

A. **Stay Calm**

DO NOT GET INTO AN ARGUMENT. Speak calmly and firmly to the person involved.

B. **Listen**

Try to accept the person's point of view.

C. **Violence Potential**

Be alert to the possibility of violence.

D. **Telephone the Public Safety Office <u>AND</u> the Crisis Response Team** (Bill Wells; Jane Rankin, ; Frank Ardaiolo; or Cindy Cassens.

Give the following information, if known:

1. The person's name.
2. The symptoms.
3. The precise location of the person (state "Library", floor, room).

E. **Be Patient**

Gain as much time as possible since the person's perception may be only temporarily distorted.

GENERAL INFORMATION

A. **Causes**

Psychiatric crises can be caused by many things ranging from scholastic pressures to drug withdrawal.

B. **Actions**

Psychiatric antagonism may be either directed against one's self or someone else; suicide, and homicide being the most extreme forms.

C. **Your Attitude**

Library personnel should always be pleasant, considerate, helpful and understanding. A mentally disturbed individual may only require a slightly abrasive experience to reduce him to desperation.

ELEVATOR FAILURE

IMMEDIATE ACTION

A. **Reassurance**

If a person is stranded in an elevator, it is important for the library's staff to give reassurance until help can be secured.

B. **Attempt to open the elevator doors.**

The elevator doors may be opened by **gently** pushing them apart. If they do not open easily, excessive force should not be used.

C. **Telephone for Help**

1. Library units should report mechanical problems to the Physical Plant Department.
2. If difficulty is encountered in getting help, call the Public Safety Office.

GENERAL INFORMATION

A. **Maintenance**

The maintenance of all library passenger elevators is the responsibility of the Elevator Company. A planned maintenance program is routinely carried out by their personnel.

B. **Keys**

Library employees normally do not have keys to the elevator motor area.

FIRE

IMMEDIATE ACTION

A. **KEEP CALM**

You help no one by panic and you may panic others.

B. **Get the People Out**--Avoid Use of Elevators

1. Pull the fire alarm. (Public Safety Office and Fire Department will automatically be alerted.) Nearest locations are:

 ____

 ____

2. Nearest fire exits are: **(see floor plans)**
3. Follow emergency evacuation plan for the library (to be developed by each unit and inserted behind this section). If safe, physically check all areas of the library for people, including:

 a. Faculty Carrels
 b. Restrooms
 c. Lounges
 d. Stairwells
 e. Elevators

4. Check for people in **wheelchairs**. Since the elevators may not be used in a fire emergency, they will have to carried down or up the stairs. Fire exits which are wheelchair accessible are: Front entrance, rear Myrtle Drive fire exit, and rear service entrance.
5. If you feel you can fight the fire, (e.g., a small one in a wastebasket) use the nearest fire extinguisher providing it is the right type. See the next page for "Instructions for Your Fire Extinguisher."
6. If safe, close all doors on your way out. Leave lights on and report to the designated person that everyone is out.
7. These procedures should be followed whenever the fire alarm sounds. Do not assume it is a drill.

C. **Call Public Safety Office Immediately**

1. Call the Public Safety Office. Report: **Exact location of fire.**
2. Meet fireman or the Public Safety Officer at the fire alarm box on the corner of Oakland Avenue and Eden Terrace.

D. **Notify the Library Administration**

Call the Library Administration. If no answer, and there is damage to materials or catalogs from fire or water, call the Dean or the Associate Dean at home.

INSTRUCTIONS FOR YOUR FIRE EXTINGUISHER

NAMEPLATE SYMBOL	TYPES OF FIRES
	For wood, paper, cloth, trash and other ordinary combustibles.

For gasoline, greases, oil, paints and other flammable liquids.

For live electrical equipment.

THE NAMEPLATE ON YOUR EXTINGUISHER SHOWS THE SYMBOLS DESIGNATING TYPES OF FIRES ON WHICH THIS EXTINGUISHER SHOULD BE USED. READ IT CAREFULLY. DO NOT USE ON CLASS D FIRES (COMBUSTIBLE METALS, E.G. MAGNESIUM)

A. **An Introduction to Your Fire Extinguisher**

Fires come in all sizes but only three basic types. They are known as Class A, Class B and Class C.

1. Class A fires are those involving paper, cloth, wood, upholstery, and other ordinary combustibles.
2. Class B fires involve gasoline, oil, grease, and other flammable liquids. Water should not be used on this type of fire.
3. Class C fires involve electrical equipment and here again water should not be used because of the danger of severe shock.

Your extinguisher is basically a storage container for a special fire extinguishing agent. When the extinguisher is operated the agent is expelled by a continuous stream of pressure stored in the container. Do not incinerate by throwing into a fire; it may explode.

Never try out the extinguisher to see if it functions unless you are prepared to completely recharge it or replace it immediately. **A partially used extinguisher will quickly lose its pressure and become useless in a few hours.**

B. **Operation**

Operation instructions and cautions for this extinguisher are printed on the nameplate. Read and understand these before a fire occurs.

Most types of fire extinguishers discharge their contents in 8 to 25 seconds depending upon size. It is therefore important that the extinguisher be aimed correctly at the fire before it is operated.

Be prepared for the discharge. There will be a slight backward reaction as the agent is being discharged from the nozzle or horn.

Stand 6 to 10 feet away from the fire and aim at the base of the flames with a side to side sweeping motion across the width of the fire. Move closer as the fire is extinguished. You are too close if the discharge disturbs the burning material. If possible, keep the wind behind you. After the fire appears to be out, continue to watch for "flashbacks" and extinguish them immediately.

Have the extinguishers recharged as soon as possible.

(Note: The preceding text has been excerpted from the *Owner's Instruction Manual*, Amerex Corp., Trussville, Alabama.)

FIRST AID

IMMEDIATE ACTION

A. **Trained Persons**

Persons trained in first aid in this library are:

Circulation staff

B. **First Aid**

Get this assistance of someone in your area who has taken first aid training courses. If you do not know how to administer first aid, you may do more harm than good.

C. **Call Public Safety Office**

If someone has been injured and is in need of emergency help, call the Public Safety Office. They have mobile equipment. Report:

1. The problem.
2. The exact location (state "Library", floor, room).
3. Your name.
4. Have someone meet them at the door.

GENERAL INFORMATION

A. **Course**

First aid courses are offered by the Red Cross. It is recommended that if you have not taken a Red Cross First Aid course, or if it has been some time since you have taken such a course, you avail yourself of the opportunity.

B. **First Aid Kits**

First Aid Kits must be maintained in a ready state by a person in the department charged with this responsibility.

C. **Good Samaritan Law**

South Carolina state law protects "Good Samaritans" from lawsuits.

§15-1-310. Liability for emergency care rendered at scene of accident.

Any person, who in good faith gratuitously renders emergency care at the scene of an accident or emergency to the victim thereof, shall not be liable for any civil damages for any personal injury as a result of any act or omission by such person in rendering the emergency care or as a result of any act or failure to act to provide or arrange for further medical treatment or care for the injured person, except acts or omission amounting to gross negligence or willful or wanton misconduct.

FLOODING AND WATER LEAKS

IMMEDIATE ACTION

A. **Stay Out**

DO NOT ENTER THE FLOODED AREA UNTIL PHYSICAL PLANT ELECTRICIANS HAVE DISCONNECTED THE ELECTRICITY--THERE IS EXTREME DANGER OF SHOCK.

B. **Guard**

Post a staff member at the entrance to the flooded area to keep out unauthorized personnel.

C. **Telephone**

1. Public Safety Office
2. Physical Plant
3. Winthrop College Library Administration. If no answer, call the Dean of Library Services or the Associate Dean at home.

D. **Salvage**

Find location to which water-soaked books and records can be transferred. It should:

1. Be adequately ventilated.
2. Have easy access to exterior of building, be above the ground floor and be serviced by an elevator.
3. Be entirely isolated from other library collections and in an area containing no rugs or other floor coverings that might be damaged by water.

FOLLOW-UP

A. **Pumping**

Have water pumped out by the fire department with the advice of the Physical Plant.

B. When the area has been declared safe by the Public Safety Office, remove the library material in the following order:

1. Material designated by departments as important in the attached appendix.
2. Undamaged library material in the immediate vicinity of the flooding (try to remove and keep in proper shelving order).
3. Damaged library material.

C. Beyond the three above steps, do not attempt further emergency treatment but await further instructions from assigned library personnel.

WATER LEAKS

IMMEDIATE ACTION

A. Move material out of the area affected.

B. Cover affected area with plastic and/or wastebaskets.

C. Contact Physical Plant Department.

FUMES (POSSIBLY TOXIC)

IMMEDIATE ACTION

A. **Suspicion of Toxic Fumes**

1. If the presence of possibly toxic fumes is suspected, clear the area.
2. Call Public Safety Office.

a. Describe the situation.
b. Give the location (state "Library", floor, room).
c. Give your name.

B. **Treatment**

Remove any person showing symptoms of a problem from the contaminated area. If necessary, give mouth-to-mouth resuscitation and/or treat for shock.

GENERAL INFORMATION

A. **Inspection**

Problems of fume danger can be partially avoided by regular and routine inspection of the library unit. Look for various types of mechanical equipment, stored chemicals, etc.

Particular care should be taken of the air intakes outside of buildings. Gasoline motors can have their exhaust fumes sucked into the building.

INSECT BITES

IMMEDIATE ACTION

A. **Watch for Allergic Reactions**

1. The reaction may come on quickly or slowly. When someone has been bitten, look for signs of difficulty in breathing, or severe chest pains, severe swelling or blotchy appearance in the area of the sting.
2. Ask the person bitten if they have had previous bad reactions.

B. **Call Public Safety Office**

If an allergic reaction appears to be taking place, call Public Safety Office immediately. Give details on location and cause of problem. Describe the reaction. The Public Safety Office has emergency equipment.

C. **First Aid** (trained personnel only)

For even mild or normal reactions.

1. Give black coffee.
2. Apply ice or cold water on the bite.

GENERAL INFORMATION

A. Encourage all staff with known allergic reactions to know what should be done for them and carry any medication that is necessary.

B. The most severe reactions may be caused by stings directly into the bloodstream and stings of the mouth or throat tissue. In the latter case, the throat may close and the person cannot breathe.

C. Generally, if a person has been bitten it might be suggested they call a doctor if they have <u>any</u> concern whatever.

MACHINERY AND EQUIPMENT

Winthrop College
Disaster Manual

GENERAL INFORMATION

A. **Causes**

The causes of problems with machinery and equipment fall into four categories.

1. Fire.
2. Shock.
3. Mechanical Crushing.
4. Fumes.

Do whatever is necessary in terms of first aid, fire extinguishing, etc. as an immediate measure.

B. **Inspection**

Routine inspection of the condition of equipment is the best way to avoid problems. In certain cases, inspection can be made only by authorized personnel. In the case of air conditioning or other heavy equipment, Physical Plant personnel will be required.

MEDICAL PROBLEMS

IMMEDIATE ACTION

A. **Unconscious Person**

Do not presume death has occurred.

B. **Call Public Safety Office Immediately**

Telephone Public Safety Office, give them the following information, and remain on the telephone until released.

1. Description of the situation.
2. Exact location (state "Library", floor, room).
3. Your name.

C. **First Aid**

1. Appropriate emergency first aid should be given by a trained person. (CPR or other appropriate aid).
2. Look for "Medic Alert" type tag with standard Physician's symbol. This may be located around the arm, neck or in a wallet. This would indicate special medical problems.

Standard Bracelet

M A
E L
D E
I R
C T

D. **Notify the Library Administration**

The appropriate administrator should be notified.

E. **Death**

If death is confirmed the Public Safety Office will notify the appropriate College Office. That Office will notify the next of kin.

F. **Precautionary Measures**

Staff members with serious medical problems should be encouraged to notify their supervisor and co-workers of their medical problems as well as any standard emergency treatment related to that problem.

POWER FAILURE

IMMEDIATE ACTION

A. **Safety**

In the case of a power failure, the first concern of the staff is for the safety of the people in the library. If the power failure is prolonged, standard evacuation procedures should be followed. Elevators, wash-rooms and stair wells should be checked for stranded persons.

B. **Call Public Safety**

Call the Public Safety Office and describe the situation.

C. **Operations**

If the failure occurs during the daytime hours, there may be sufficient natural light to continue library operations. However, in many cases during daylight, and in all cases at night, the library should be evacuated if the failure is expected to continue for an extended period of time.

D. **Extended Failure**

If the failure is to be extended, the Dean of Library Services should be notified. It is her responsibility to make the decision on continued library operations.

GENERAL INFORMATION

A. **Auxiliary Lighting**

Each individual library unit and each floor of the library should have auxiliary lighting to be used in case of a power failure, even if this lighting is only in the form of flashlights. Staff members should be familiar with the location of flashlights and emergency lights.

B. **Flashlights**

Routine monthly checks should be made to be certain that:

1. The flashlights are still there.
2. They are in first class operating condition.

TORNADO WARNING PROCEDURES

GENERAL PURPOSE

Winthrop College
Disaster Manual

The purpose of this memorandum is to establish the policy and procedures to be followed by the student body, faculty, and staff in the event of a tornado warning alert or actual tornado. Through the implementation of these procedures when necessary, it should minimize disruption of scheduled activities, injury, and loss of life.

Tornado Alert

In the event of a tornado alert, the Winthrop College Community will be advised immediately by alert siren and by the Public Safety Officer using the public address system in each Public Safety vehicle. Then, depending on where we are, the action to be taken will be decided as outlined in the general instructions below.

In any given twenty-four (24) hour time period, the Winthrop College Community would be located in one or more of the following areas:

Classrooms
Residence Halls
Staff Officers
Outside on campus grounds

A. **CLASSROOMS**

In the event that a tornado alert is sounded during class periods, the professor conducting the class will be responsible to move the students away from windows to/near an inside wall. If time allows, the professor should move the students in his/her class to the lowest floor possible, and as stated before, they should attempt to locate themselves near an inside wall. It is imperative that all those involved remain inside the building for maximum protection.

B. **RESIDENCE HALLS**

The Resident Director's and RA's will be responsible to notify all students under their direction who are in the respective dorms at the time of the tornado alert and to move the students to an inside wall away from windows. If time allows the students should locate themselves near an inside wall on the lowest floor of the building. It is imperative that the students be advised to remain inside the building for maximum protection.

C. **STAFF OFFICES**

The staff of Winthrop College, upon receiving word of a tornado alert, should leave their work stations and locate themselves on the lowest floor of the respective buildings. In all cases they should attempt to move away from windows and near an inside wall. It is imperative that all staff employees remain inside to minimize injury and loss of life.

D. **OUTSIDE ON CAMPUS GROUNDS**

If at anytime you are outside and hear a tornado alert, or see a tornado and do not have time to locate yourself inside a building, then the next alternative is to lie flat in the nearest depression such as a ditch, curb or ravine.

E. **RESPONSIBILITY TO NOTIFY OF TORNADO ALERT PROCEDURE**

It will be the responsibility of each school dean and the Dean of Students to advise the people in their respective area of their responsibility to the Winthrop College Community in case of a tornado alert.

DISASTER PREPAREDNESS COMMITTEE

This committee will meet at least two times a year to review procedures and information. Any changes of names, phone numbers or experts agreeing to help will be reported immediately to the chairman so emergency information can be updated.

Winthrop College
Disaster Manual

The committee will work in two areas of interest: Disaster Prevention and Disaster Recovery.

A. **Disaster Prevention**

1. Check equipment, manuals and problem areas regularly.
2. Keep the Emergency Manual updated, including names and telephone numbers.
3. Locate sources of emergency supplies e.g. milk crates, trucks, dehumidifiers, fans.
4. Locate emergency facilities such as freezers, vacuum dry facilities.
5. Inform Public Safety Office of plans and provide an emergency manual for their information, along with a list of names and phone numbers.
6. Distribute revisions to the emergency manual as needed to all concerned parties.
7. Arrange continuing education for all Library personnel.

B. **Disaster Recovery**

1. Notify all concerned people as events happen, e.g. (Public Safety Office, fire department, police, and library administration).
2. Take photographs of all affected areas and materials before, during, and after recovery.
3. Appraise damage and sets up a plan of action.
4. Assign person to call for supplies first, then facilities.
5. Recovery director organizes efforts, sets up communication, call for volunteers.
6. Establish temperature and humidity controls.
7. Set up all bibliographic controls.
8. Set up teams with **pre-trained** leaders to deal with books--removing from shelves, carrying, handling, packing, etc. Train volunteers on-site.
9. Arrange needed comforts such as portable restrooms, coffee and soft drinks, towels, food, aspirin, etc.
10. Wrap up disaster steps.

Committee members:

Laurance (Larry) Mitlin
Geraldine (Geri) Gaskill
Gloria Kelley, Chairperson
Ron Chepesiuk

The Following Section Presents

Detailed Procedures for Recovery

From a Major Fire or Other Disaster

Which Involves Significant Water Damage

To the Library or Its Collections

GUIDE TO RECOVERING FROM A FIRE

(Detailed Procedures Follow This Section)

Winthrop College
Disaster Manual

Note: As soon as the fire is out and the building is declared safe to enter, the following things should occur **simultaneously**:

A. Establish the character and degree of damage. Seek the advice and help of book and paper conservators with experience. Library personnel are usually trained in this area.

B. Try to prevent further damage from water by covering areas with sheets of plastic. Move all office equipment and supplies to the center of the room. Plastic sheets should have adequate drainage so further damage will not occur. This would also include covering the roof.

C. Begin pumping water from the roof and floors.

D. Reduce high temperature and vent the areas as soon as the water has receded or been pumped out. Try to control the humidity. Turn off all heat. Bring portable fans and dehumidifiers into the building to control temperature.

E. Organize by consulting qualified people to help in establishing a plan of action. This should be handled within the first couple of hours.

F. Once a plan has been established, meet with executive officers of the college to make sure every one understands the recovery plan.

G. Meet with every one with materials in the building and explain the plan of action. This meeting should include insurance coverage for damaged materials and how their materials will be salvaged and where they would be housed. Make clear that only rare and value materials should be salvaged, even though all materials will eventually be removed from the building.

H. Make a list and photographs of the contents of the building for insurance purposes.

PLAN

NOTE: This is not the time to begin weeding. Freeze everything and then develop a systematic plan for discarding items that are beyond recovery.

A. Hire a consultant if you're not comfortable with on campus expertise. Library personnel are familiar with and trained to handle disasters.

B. Hire outside services to handle different materials. You will probably need someone to vacuum the building of water, process magnetic materials, disks, etc.

C. Divide recovery teams into groups, one to handle each form of material, furniture, books, and building, etc.

D. Remove the wettest paper items first.

E. Stabilize paper materials by freezing. **This step should occur within 48 hours for wet materials.**

F. Try to locate a local freezer locker. (See appendix)

G. Try to locate plastic containers for packing materials (milk crates or bread trays.)

H. Use other campus buildings for transferring material that is not completely wet. (Coliseum or McBryde Cafeteria). Use portable fans, hang manuscripts on nylon lines or lay flat on floors.

I. Promptly wrap materials in freezer paper, wax paper or silicone papers to prevent them from sticking together.

J. Pack crates or heavy duty boxes with books spine down, one layer deep.

K. Boxes should be marked with contents e.g. call numbers, floor number.

L. Transportation should be provided for transporting material to selected storage places. Refrigerated trucks would be better than uncovered trucks.

M. College will need to have certain supplies available and if they are not available be ready to purchase supplies for handling disaster:

Paper towels, trash liners, sponges, plastic sheeting in rolls, wax paper, freezer paper, electric fans, dehumidifiers, portable electric sump pumps . (See appendix.)

RECOVERY

A. After material is frozen, the college will need to hire a vacuum and/or freeze drying company for drying material. (See appendix)

B. Hire a company to pump entire building of moisture. (See appendix)

SALVAGE PROCEDURES FOR WATER-DAMAGED MATERIALS

A number of options are available for treating water-damaged materials. The choice of treatment will depend upon the extent and type of damage incurred, and the manpower, expertise, and facilities available.

A. **Vacuum freeze drying**

Vacuum freeze drying is the safest and most successful method, although it is also the most expensive. Materials **must** be frozen when they are placed in a sublimation chamber. This type of chamber operates under high vacuum and high heat, and turns the ice crystals in and on the frozen materials to water vapor. The vapor is then collected on a cold panel that has been chilled to at least -200 degrees F, so it cannot go back on the materials. If they are not frozen when they are put in the chamber, the materials will freeze on the outside and the water molecules on the inside will be forced through the frozen barrier as the vacuum is pulled. This action can cause the book or document to "explode."

When materials are removed from the vacuum freeze chamber, they will be **very** dry and should acclimate for at least one month before they are opened to avoid cracking the spine and/or binding (this is especially true for leather bindings). They may be placed in a high humidity room to accelerate the acclimation process, but must be monitored closely for signs of mold.

Materials so treated will **not** look like new, but will show signs of swelling and distortion. Photographs will not be damaged by this treatment, but rubber cement will dissolve and stain the pages to which it has been applied.

For a list of vacuum freeze dry facilities see the appendix.

NOTE: Vacuum drying involves the placement of wet materials in a chamber that pulls the moisture by means of a vacuum. This method is **not** recommended as the heat involved is damaging to paper (especially bound paper) and photographic materials. Microwave ovens should not be used for the same reason.

B. **Freezing**

Freezing wet materials will stabilize them and provide you with time to determine your course of action. Mold will not grow and further deterioration from water will not occur when materials are in a frozen state.

Books have been left in a freezer for ten years and successfully thawed and air-dried with no resultant damage. Freezing will also help to eliminate smoke odor from materials.

Rapid freezing is recommended to minimize damage from ice crystals (the faster the materials are frozen, the smaller the ice crystals will be). Temperatures below 15 degrees F. will freeze and dry out wet materials. If freezer space is not immediately available, and the outside temperature is below 15 degrees F., place the materials in a secure area outside. Cover them with plastic if rain or snow is expected.

FREEZING IS AN INTERMEDIATE STAGE. After materials have been removed from the freezer, they must be placed in a vacuum freeze dryer or air-dried.

C. **Air-drying**

Air-drying should be performed only in a stable environment to inhibit the growth of mold. The ideal environment for air-drying is 50-60 degrees F. and 25-35% RH. Instructions are outlined in II below. This process is **not** recommended for coated stock materials (see III below).

The following salvage procedures are recommended:

A. **Volumes to be frozen**

1. Removal

a. Clear the floors and aisles first.
b. Begin with the wettest materials. These will usually be on the lowest shelves, unless water has come in through the ceiling.
c. Dirt and mold should be removed and treated before freezing. If time does not permit these activities, dirty and/or moldy books may be frozen (mud will easily brush off when it is dry). Silt should be washed out immediately, as it is almost impossible to remove when it is dry.
d. Pack materials on-site, if possible. If not possible, remove by human chain.
e. Keep accurate records of the locations from which materials are removed.

2. Packing

a. Remove volumes from shelves in order.
b. Wrap freezer paper around each volume (waxed side next to the volume) and place in plastic crates **spine down**.
c. Pack crates one layer only, snugly enough that volumes will not slide or lean.
d. Wrap open books as found and place on top of a packed container. Do not place more than one open volume in a container. Be sure there is a freezer paper barrier between the packed volumes and the open volume to prevent staining from binding dyes.
e. If books are stuck together, do not attempt to separate them, but pack them as one volume.
f. Pack items in the condition in which they are found. DO NOT ATTEMPT TO CLOSE OPEN VOLUMES OR OPEN CLOSED VOLUMES THAT ARE WET.

3. Record-keeping

a. Label each container with your institution's name and assign it a number.
b. On a separate sheet of paper, record the box number, call numbers of the first and last volumes packed, and the total number of books in each container.
c. If the containers are sent to more than one freezer, note which container numbers are sent where.

4. Transporting

a. Materials should be placed in a freezer facility as quickly as possible to prevent the growth of mold. Care should be taken that containers do not fall over during transport, as further damage may result.

b. Materials should be placed in refrigerated trucks if they cannot be frozen within forty-eight hours.

B. **Volumes to be air-dried**

1. Washing procedure (to be performed off-site only)

   a. Keep the book tightly closed and hold it under cold clean running water.
   b. Remove as much mud as possible from the binding by dabbing gently with a sponge. Do not rub or use brushes and do **not** sponge the pages or edges, as these actions can force the mud into the spine or the wet pages, causing further damage to the volume. Let the motion of the running water clean off the dirt.

   NOTE: A more extensive washing procedure, involving a series of rust-proof containers, may be used instead.

   c. Squeeze the book gently and with even pressure to remove excess water and to reshape the binding.
   d. Do **NOT** wash:

      open or swollen volumes
      vellum or parchment bindings or pages
      full or partial leather bindings
      fragile or brittle materials
      works of art on paper
      water-soluble components (inks, tempera, water-colors, dyes, charcoal, etc.)
      manuscripts
      non-paper materials

2. Saturated volumes

   a. DO NOT OPEN -- wet paper tears easily!
   b. Set volumes on their heads on absorbent paper. Pages tend to droop within the binding when a volume is shelved upright, so setting it on its head will counteract this tendency. Plastic sheeting should be placed under the paper toweling or unprinted newsprint to protect table tops. Turn the volumes right side up when changing the paper beneath them. Their position should be reversed each time the paper is changed and the wet paper removed from the area.
   c. Covers may be opened to support the volume.
   d. Aluminum foil may be placed between the cover and the endleaf to prevent staining from the binding dyes.
   e. When most of the water has drained, proceed as for "Damp volumes."

3. Damp volumes

   a. Very carefully open the book (not more than a 30 degree angle).
   b. Begin interleaving from the back and keep the volume in an upright position.
   c. Place interleaving sheets at intervals of twenty-five leaves (fifty pages), unless they will distort the volume.
   d. Change interleaving frequently. Do **not** reuse unless the sheets are being impregnated with fungicide. Ortho-Phenyl Phenol (O-PP) has been found to be less toxic than thymol and is recommended. Mix one pound of O-PP to one gallon of acetone or ethanol (do not use methanol, as it will cause inks to bleed). Safety equipment (mask, eye goggles, and rubber gloves) should be worn when preparing and using this solution.
   e. Continue to change the paper underneath and remove from the area.

4. Slightly damp volumes/Volumes with only wet edges

a. Stand volume on its head and fan open slightly. Paperback books may support each other with a barrier between them or they may be wedged with styrofoam pieces. Position volumes in the path of circulating air.

b. When almost dry, lay the volumes flat and place weights (not other drying books) on them to minimize distortion. DO NOT STACK WET VOLUMES.

c. Lightweight volumes (less than six pounds) may be hung on lines to dry.

Use monofilament nylon lines, not more than 1/32" diameter, not more than five or six feet long, spaced approximately one-half inch apart.
Do **not** line-dry a saturated volume as the monofilament will cut through the wet paper.

C. **Volumes with coated stock paper**

Wet coated stock paper should be handled with care, as the print will slide off the wet page if it is rubbed. Do **not** allow wet books with coated stock paper to dry in a closed state as the pages will permanently bond together. Almost all attempts to separate stuck pages by rewetting them have failed. McDonnell's Document Reclamation Service reports that vacuum freeze drying of coated stock volumes is rarely successful. Keep volumes submerged until the pages can be separated (see IV.B below). The only chance of saving such materials is to interleave **every page** and air-dry.

D. **Documents/Unbound materials**

1. Freeze as found

a. Do not remove from file cabinet drawers, document cases, or folders.

b. Do not turn containers upside down to empty or drain.

2. Separation of wet sheets

a. Place a sheet of polyester film on top of a stack of wet, unbound papers (or the first page of a bound volume).

b. Rub gently with a bone folder--surface friction will cause the wet paper to adhere to the film.

c. Peel back the top sheet and place it on top of a piece of polyester web.

d. Remove the polyester film.

e. Place another piece of polyester web on top of the wet sheet.

f. Repeat the entire process, separating the wet sheets one at a time and interleaving them with polyester web. (Materials may be frozen at this stage.)

g. Air-dry the sheets (supported by the polyester web) by placing them on absorbent paper on tables or on top of closely spaced monofilament lines. Air in the room should be kept circulating, but fans should **not** blow directly on the materials.

h. The papers may be flattened when they are almost dry by placing them between two sheets of blotting paper (to remove excess moisture) and applying even pressure with weights.

E. **Non-book materials**

1. Photographic materials (prints, negatives, slides, film)

Do not expect to salvage color photographs, as the colored layers will separate and the dyes will fade quickly. However, if you wish to try, freeze them immediately, or transport them to a photographic laboratory.

Photographic materials should not be allowed to dry out after they become wet as they will stick to their envelopes or to each other. Any attempt to separate them after they have dried together will result in damage to the emulsion or the image. Remove the materials from their protective enclosures and wash off any mud or dirt under cold, clean running water.

The following options are available for salvaging photographic materials:

a. Air-dry either flat or on lines of monofilament (plastic spring-type clothespins may be used to hang them on the lines).

b. If there are too many to air-dry, they may be stored in cold water (65 degrees F or below--cold helps to preserve the emulsion). Ice may be added to the water, but do <u>not</u> add dry ice or allow the materials to remain under water longer than three days.

   Formaldehyde may be added to the water (fifteen milliliters to one liter) to help prevent the gelatin from swelling and softening. Black and white film could last three days in this solution before the emulsion begins to separate; color film could last forty-eight hours.

   Transport the materials (in sealed polyethylene bags inside plastic garbage pails) to a professional laboratory within twenty-four hours, if possible.

c. If time does not permit air-drying, the materials may be frozen. As the emulsion may be damaged by the formation of ice crystals, freezing as quickly as possible is recommended (smaller ice crystals will cause less damage). Negatives should be separated before freezing as they tend to stick together when thawed.

d. The Eastman Kodak Company provides free emergency service for cleaning and drying its own black-and-white film. They will work on other brands of film for cost.

2. Microforms

   a. Silver halide microfilm

      Keep under water (see V.A.2 above).
      Send to Kodak or a professional microprocessing laboratory.

   b. Vesicular and diazo microfilm

      Wash off mud or dirt under cold, clean running water.
      Air-dry or dry with cheesecloth.

   c. Microfiche

      Treat the same as silver halide microfilm.
      Kodak will not treat microfiche, so send them to a professional microprocessing laboratory.

3. Tapes (audio, video, computer) and floppy disks

   Water is especially damaging to magnetic materials. The longer they have been wet, the greater the damage will be. Do **not** attempt to play any damaged tapes or disks, as they can damage the equipment on which they are being played. The following procedures are recommended if you wish to attempt to salvage tapes:

   a. Break open the cassettes.
   b. Wash in clean or distilled water.
   c. Air-dry or dry with cheesecloth.

4. Sound recordings (disks)

   Clean water probably will not damage sound recordings, but flood water carries silt, which will scratch a disk. Disks should be washed and dried with cheesecloth or a soft, lint-free cloth. Record jackets or paper protective sleeves should be discarded as they can trap moisture and may develop mold.

F. **Mold**

Mold and mildew are interchangeable terms for fungi. They can never be killed and can remain dormant for many years. Spores are always present in the air and will grow when the environment is warm and humid. Freezing will inhibit the growth of mold and is recommended if time does not permit immediate treatment.

1. Mold can develop within forty-eight to seventy-two hours in an environment where the temperature is over 75 degrees F and the relative humidity is over 60%.
2. Separate the affected materials to prevent spreading.
3. If the materials are wet and mold is beginning to develop, interleave the volumes with papers impregnated with a fungicide (see II.C.4).
4. Keep the air circulating in the room.
5. Mold is easier to remove when it is dry. Vacuum or brush it off and remove the spores from the area.
6. Materials that will be fumigated should be removed from plastic crates, as plastic will absorb the fumigants. Fungicidal fogging should be done only by a professional chemist or conservator.

G. DO **NOT**, UNDER ANY CIRCUMSTANCES,

...enter an area until it has been declared safe.
...attempt to open a wet book (one tear costs at least one dollar to mend!).
...attempt to close an open book that is swollen.
...use mechanical presses on wet materials.
...attempt to separate books that are stuck together.
...write on wet paper.
...use bleaches, detergents, water-soluble fungicides, adhesive tapes (or adhesives of any kind), paper clips, or staples on wet materials.
...use colored paper of any kind during salvage and recovery operations.
...pack newly-dried materials in boxes or leave them unattended for more than two days.

CLEANING SMOKE DAMAGED MATERIALS

NOTE: Make sure material is dry before trying to clean smoke damaged material. If material is not dry, see Salvage Procedures for Water-Damaged Materials.

A. If soot has accumulated on the material, try vacuum cleaning. Lightly run the vacuum over the material making sure not to further damage the material.

B. If soot is still on the material, try using a white vinyl eraser (can be obtained from Servicemaster). When using the eraser or sponge, use one way strokes only.

C. To get rid of the smoke smell, first make sure the area is well ventilated.

D. Place baking soda or charcoal briquettes in container and let stand a few days to help absorb the smell.

MATERIALS TO BE SAVED IN THE EVENT OF A DISASTER

PUBLIC SERVICES

NOTE: See floor plans in the appendix for exact location of all necessary materials.

Circulation Department

A. Remove all tape cartridges located in black metal cabinet in corner of computer room. Computer room is located in the Technical Services area on the first floor.

Documents Department

A. Latest "List of Classes" notebook and "Items Selected" notebook. Located on the worktable in the Documents

Office on the second floor.

B. Documents Department Manual, Instructions to Depository Libraries Manual and Federal Depository Library Manual. All manuals are located on file cabinet behind librarian's desk.

C. Computer Disks. Located on Apple Computer Cart in the Documents Office on the second floor.

Reference Department

A. Inter-library loan Active Transaction File, File of computer disks, ILL Logs (three large clipboards), and ILL Books Borrowed from other libraries. All files are located by typewriter on ILL Desk.

B. Copyright file. Four boxes located on right side of ILL desk with blue forms.

Archives and Special Collections

A. Inventory Books, Donor Control Files and Card Catalog. Located in room 14A.

B. Personnel Records, Round of Trustee Minutes, Theses, Presidents Papers. Located in room 14.

C. Clan Collections membership files and rare books. Located in room 8 and 9.

D. Alumni Records. Located in room 2.

E. Pueblo, Picasso, Truman Capote, Alex, and Mexican Ornithology. Located in room 19

F. Clay Tablets, Washington Letter, and Lincoln letter. Located in Librarian's office.

TECHNICAL SERVICES

1. All tapes located in black metal cabinet in corner of computer room in technical services.

ADDITIONAL SERVICES

Fire Department

Public Safety Office

Crawford Health Center

Motor Pool

Piedmont Medical Center
Ambulance Service

Carpenter
Electrician
Plumber
Exterminator — Physical Plant
Locksmith
Utility company
Janitorial Services

CONSULTANTS

Lisa Fox **--FIRST CONTACT**
Director
SOLINET Preservation Program

Ms. Sarah (Sally) Buchanan

Karen Motylewski
Field Service Director
Northeast Document Conservation Center

Document Reprocessors
Eric Lundquist---contact person

Vacuum freeze-drying (Has a mobile unit on the east coast)

Carlisle Memory Products
Kevin Burton - contact person

Handles data recovery (computer disks)

Moisture Control Services Atlanta Office

Handles humidity control, drying buildings, furnishings and damp library materials.

McDonnell Aircraft Company
Fred Brodbeck—Contact person only at the last result.

Thermal drying

Library of Congress
Shandura Shahani or
Dr. Robert McComb
Peter Waters

Solex Technology
Don Hartsell, President

Provides on-site humidity control and drying of buildings, furnishings, and collections.

Blackmon-Mooring-Steamatic Catastrophe
Pat Moore or
Tommie Stanley—Contact persons

Provides assistance in salvage of water and smoke/fire damaged materials.

Reoda Chemical Engineering
Skip McLaughting—Contact person

Provides cleaning and deodorizing service. They do not provide on-site work. Work is done in the Ohio office.

LIST OF SUPPLIES AND EQUIPMENT

Paper towels
Trash liners
Sponges (regular and white vinyl)
Mops
Pails
Plastic Sheeting (rolls)
Masking tape
Wax paper (rolls)
Gloves, plastic or rubber
Brooms
Electric fans
Dehumidifiers
Portable electric sump pump
Extension cords (heavy duty)
Polyester film
Cheese cloth
Erasers (white vinyl)

Physical Plant may have some of the above supplies.

Milk crates, plastic	Coble Dairy Products
	Kraft Inc. Diary Group
	Pet Diary Group
	Hunter Jersey Farms
	Peeler's Dairy

Bread trays

Cold Storage freezers	Sowell's Meat and Services
	United Refrigerated Co.
	McBryde Cafeteria

EMERGENCY NUMBERS

Some member of the Library Administration should be notified of any emergency as soon as possible. If the Dean of Library Services is unavailable, one of the following persons should be contacted:

PAUL Z. DUBOIS	Dean of Library Services
LAURANCE R. MITLIN	Associate Dean of Library Services
ROBERT GORMAN	Head, Public Services Division
GLORIA KELLEY	Head, Technical Services Division

ADDITIONAL EMERGENCY NUMBERS

MARGARET JORDAN	Director, Public Safety
WALTER HARDIN	Director, Physical Plant
LARRY KITHCART	Supply Manager
ANTHONY DIGIORGIO	President
DAN PANTALEO	Vice President for Academic Affairs and Dean of the Faculty
J. P. MCKEE	Vice President for Business and Finance

DISASTER PREPAREDNESS COMMITTEE

LAURANCE MITLIN

GLORIA KELLEY

GERALDINE GASKILL

RONALD CHEPESIUK

AT ANY HOUR call Physical Plant Operations

Report any failures in building services, or electric, water, heating, or gas failures or breaks, of fallen trees or wires to the Physical Plant Operations.

Disaster Preparedness Planning for North Dakota Libraries

North Dakota Library Association

1987

Forward and Acknowledgements

The Disaster Preparedness Committee was established in response to a growing realization on the part of North Dakota's library community that planning for a proper response to emergencies was needed. The intent of this manual is not to provide a plan but rather to provide procedures and an outline for planning. In developing this manual, the committee reviewed a number of manuals done by others; too many, unfortunately, to give adequate recognition for the ideas they may have provided or even to properly recall from whence they came. In part this is due to the fact that most such manuals are very similar both because of the nature of the topic and because of the library community's generous willingness to freely share thoughts and ideas.

We would especially thank Toby Murray, Archivist and Preservation Officer, University of Tulsa, for her review of and thoughtful comments on a draft of this manual. We also thank her for allowing us to reproduce, with some modifications, her bibliography and the section of this manual dealing with salvage procedures.

In addition to the chairperson, the original committee included Tom Jones, Veterans Memorial Public Library, Bismarck; and John Bye, North Dakota State University, Institute for Regional Studies. A second committee, which reviewed the draft manual, included Donna Maston, Veterans Memorial Public Library, Bismarck; Lotte Bailey, University of Mary Library, Bismarck; Ivan Opp, Stanley Public Schools, Stanley; and Jim Robbins, Veterans Administration Center Library, Fargo.

Gerald G. Newborg, Chairperson
Disaster Preparedness Committee

DISASTER PREPAREDNESS PLANNING FOR NORTH DAKOTA LIBRARIES

North Dakota Library Association
Disaster Preparedness Committee
1987

Table of Contents

I. INTRODUCTION TO DISASTER PREPAREDNESS

Contrary to some people's fears, preparing for disaster doesn't invite disaster. In fact, the opposite is more often the case. Yet the same reluctance which causes wills to go unwritten, or medical checkups delayed, also has us put off preparing for contingencies we do not want to consider. Other factors are at work as well, of course. Priorities are often set by those demands which seem most pressing. Disasters are only recognized, only exist, after they occur. This manual urges North Dakota's library community to plan for these very possible, if unthinkable, occurrences. Rather than answer all possible questions, its objective is to prompt the questions which should be asked - and answered. An individual plan must still be developed by each library.

There are three components of disaster preparedness that this short manual aims to address. First, and most important, is disaster prevention. While it is impossible to guard against all potential emergencies, some things can be prevented by regular inspection and preventive action. At minimum, librarians and records custodians should be aware of the potential for damage and the consequences of inaction.

A second component, an extension of the first, is damage minimization. Steps can be taken which will help control damage in the event of a disaster. Part of this component of disaster preparedness is the identification of key materials or key information which can be provided special protection or which can be used when responding to an emergency situation.

The third and final component is establishing a plan for reacting to an emergency. Should disaster strike, the speed and manner of response is often crucial. Knowing who will assume particular responsibilities, where certain expertise may be found, and where to obtain needed supplies and services can make the difference between minor and major disaster.

Disaster Prevention

Disaster need not take the form of nuclear war or destruction by a tornado. While tornados are very real possibilities in North Dakota, a frozen water pipe or overheated space heater may be a more likely occurrence. Librarians need to know what form disaster may take in order to adequately prepare for it. Lax enforcement of smoking rules or an office copier located in a stack area will cause more fires than will lightning. Disaster prevention is based on looking at your facilities and procedures and determining what can be done to prevent damage to the facilities, collections, patrons and staff. Do you have and do you enforce rules relating to smoking? Is electrical equipment located away from flammable materials and in a supervised area? Office copiers can be dangerous. Has the building's electrical system been inspected recently and are staff instructed on the dangers of overloading outlets or of using light-duty extension cords? Has the roof of the building been inspected for leaks, do the drains in the basement work, can the sewers back up, are the gutters and downspouts clear? Water spilling over a clogged gutter down through a broken basement window will cause the same damage as the water from a river overflowing its banks.

Disaster Minimization

Concurrent with evaluating facilities and procedures for disaster prevention, librarians should seek to minimize problems which may occur. In effect, this is attempting to prevent a minor problem from escalating into a major disaster. For example, should a fire occur there are many potential ways of increasing the likelihood that the fire can be contained or put out before extensive damage takes place. In all cases there are costs and potential benefits to consider. A fire suppression system such as sprinklers, 24-hour security monitoring, fire alarms tied into the local fire department, ready access to fire extinguishers and staff training in their use, and compartmentalization of the structure with additional fire walls are all means which can be used to minimize the damage from a fire. All have costs attached to them, of course, as well as additional considerations relating to minimizing damage. The result of putting out a paper fire with water is wet paper, but the damage which results may vary considerably. For example, fire hoses can be adapted to do less damage by use of a nozzle which produces a fine mist rather than a stream. Sprinkler system lines can include monitors which sound an alarm when water moves in the pipes. Disaster minimization requires the same care and planning as disaster prevention.

Disaster minimization is also a part of disaster response, as described below. Minimization of the effects of a disaster results from prior planning and quick response. Ask yourself what is vital to your operation. Computer records of shelf lists have, for many libraries, minimized one area of concern. Look at your collections. What will you be unable to replace? You may wish to microfilm (or even duplicate on an office copier) certain records which are vital to your operation and store the copies off-site. In addition, certain areas of the building may be more or less susceptible to damage. Collections and records may be stored accordingly.

Disaster Response

Although it is difficult to convince governing bodies of the fact, the costs of disaster prevention and disaster minimization are minor compared to the costs of replacing or salvaging books and records. However, sometimes even the best efforts of librarians will not prevent a disaster from occurring. Furthermore, none of us have the power to prevent a tornado or other natural disaster that might overtake us. As noted above, any disaster response plan depends upon what types of catastrophies might occur. Only after we have in mind what we might face will we be able to properly prepare our response. It would be well to compile a list of all possibilities and attach some concept of probability to each. Tornado, lightning, flood, arson, and vandalism are all possibilities for most libraries. As these are analyzed, however, the most significant possibility for damage is water and the effects of fire. Preparation for responding to a disaster, therefore, must always include how to salvage water-damaged materials.

North Dakota Library Association

The first step in disaster response is to assemble a team of staff members who will participate in establishing a plan and who will have clearly assigned responsibilities in case of an emergency and who will be the primary architects of your plan to prevent or minimize damage. The team roster is the first element of a disaster plan. It includes names and telephone numbers, who is in charge, and who is second in command should the team leader be unavailable. Alternates should be designated for team members should any of them be unavailable.

II. DEVELOPING A DISASTER PLAN

What are you preparing for?

What you are preparing for has some effect on the type of preparations you make. While seemingly obvious, the differences may be more of degree than of type. For example, you may conclude that a vital library record should be protected through duplication so that, should disaster strike, the duplicate record can be retrieved and business resumed. Where do you store the duplicate record? If you are preparing for incoming enemy missiles, your answer may be "far away and underground." If you are preparing for a flood, your answer should not include another institution in the same flood plain. If you are preparing against vandalism, a second copy in a back office may be adequate. Part of preparation is assessing possibility and probability. North Dakota has severe winters and broken water pipes are always a possibility. What would happen if a water pipe burst? Would you know about it if it happened at night or if you were not in the immediate area? These are the questions you must ask yourself as you begin to construct your disaster plan.

Available staff and resources.

Many organizations in our state do not have the wide range of experts which we would like to fill out our team. That does not necessarily mean that such expertise is not available. In addition to your local fire department, who should tour your facility in any case, you may wish to seek the advice of qualified electricians, plumbers, architects or other knowledgeable individuals to help analyze your facility for potential problems. Include the names, addresses and telephone numbers of these individuals in your disaster plan for quick reference when your pipes burst or your fuses blow. Being able to contact someone who is already familiar with your facility is an advantage. In addition, be aware of available expertise, equipment, and other resources in other organizations in your area or elsewhere in the state. List these items in your plan for ready reference. Most importantly, become aware of available information on this subject. Read, starting with some of the materials in the bibliography below, so that you can effectively establish and implement a disaster plan for your facility.

What do you want to save?

This question has already been raised, but not adequately answered. First and foremost, you want to save lives. Not all disasters strike in the night, so any disaster plan should include steps for evacuating staff and visitors and for assuring that all are safe. Preparation for tornados includes location of suitable shelter and an orderly means for reaching it. Minimizing loss does NOT include risking personal injury to save or salvage materials. Such efforts are done as preparation before any disaster strikes or as a salvage effort after the physical danger is past. Beyond this, what are you insured against? What can or will insurance replace? Salvaging current best sellers may cost more than replacing them. Rare books or office records may be irreplaceable. In addition, knowing what you lost may be a prerequisite for recovering damages from your insurance company.

Proper identification of what you want to save can come only from assigning priorities to these materials and locating them on floor plans which in turn are a part of your disaster plan. These floor plans will contain other information as well, such as location of exits, evacuation routes, location of emergency supplies, fire extinguishers, alarms, and other necessary information. For each area of the library and for supplies, equipment, furnishings, collections and records, ask the following questions:

Can this be replaced and, if so, at what cost?

How important is this item? (You may not need to replace it at all.)

Is this item available elsewhere and of such little reference use that it need not be available here?

Would the cost of replacement be more or less than the cost of salvage and restoration?

Where do you start?

As noted above, the assembling of a team and assigning of responsibilities is the initial step in establishing a disaster preparedness plan. Depending upon the expertise of available individuals, and the number of people available, this may be a complex or lonely task. Larger organizations may want to establish committees or task forces to deal with particular areas. Smaller libraries may want to seek outside review of their plan, particularly for areas in which they lack confidence. Large or small, however, someone must be given authority to act quickly and to direct operations in the event of an emergency, including authority to allocate funds. Each member of the team can be given specific responsibilities for both emergency operations and for more routine tasks relating to disaster avoidance. After the plan is completed, you will want it and the responsibilities that go with it to be ratified by your organization's governing body so that staff will have clear authority to act should an emergency arise.

Having received their assignments, members of the team will want to assemble as much information as possible, including additional information on disaster preparedness and about their particular assignments; floor plans for locating equipment, supplies, records, collections, and evacuation routes; and information on needed supplies, equipment, and services.

What is active prevention?

Prevention is not a one-time procedure, but is an ongoing process. Deterioration continues, equipment malfunctions, staff changes. Prevention activities should therefore be scheduled and written procedures established to ensure compliance. For example, you may establish routines for daily, weekly, monthly, quarterly, semi-annual, and annual inspections. Daily you will want to ensure that aisles and work areas are free of clutter and debris, that smoking regulations are enforced, that all materials are stored off the floor, and so forth. You may set up a monthly routine to check the operability of smoke and water alarms, flashlights, radios, and other similar items. Gutters, downspouts, windows and skylights might be on a semi-annual inspection list, while roofs and furnaces might be on an annual inspection list. Some items, such as the general electrical system, may be reviewed even less frequently, but it is important to establish specific schedules for all these items to ensure that timely inspections will be done. Further, responsibility for inspections should be specifically assigned in writing (as part of your plan), checklists established, and for other than daily inspections, checklists completed and filed to document activities. See Appendix A for a suggested list of items to incorporate into your checklists.

What do you need?

Planning for potential disaster includes knowing where to turn in time of need - quickly. Time is precious. If you have wet materials and temperatures are above 70 degrees, mold will begin to form within 48 hours. Salvaging books and records depends upon making the right decisions quickly and having the appropriate resources available. Staff should be familiar with the publication _Procedures for Salvage of Water-Damaged Library Materials_ by Peter Waters (Library of Congress: Washington, 1979). This brief publication provides concise and accurate information on how to proceed in a salvage effort. This should be must reading for all librarians. With that and other information resources as a basis for salvage procedures, you will want access to the following:

Space. Air drying, cleaning and other salvage operations require extensive space and good air circulation. In the event of extensive damage, a warehouse or gymnasium may be sought. In fair weather, you may be able to do some work out of doors, but only if the temperature, humidity and wind cooperate.

Plastic garbage cans or other rustproof receptacles. Mud can be cleaned from already wet volumes by washing if great care is taken and if the salvage team is knowledgeable concerning paper types.

Cardboard boxes or plastic crates, such as those used for carrying milk cartons or those used as organizers in the home, are needed for transporting materials and for holding books for air drying.

Commercial freezer space may be needed for freezing water-damaged materials until salvage can be performed. In winter, unheated buildings will be adequate for this purpose.

Plastic bags and waxed paper are used for wrapping and interleaving materials prior to freezing.

Plastic sheeting is needed for protecting material. Because of the value of plastic sheeting for quick, temporary protection, there should always be a roll on hand in a designated location. Scissors and tape should be stored with it.

UNPRINTED newsprint (the ink from printed newsprint may rub off onto wet materials) can be used for blotting or interleaving.

White paper towels are used for cleaning and blotting (dyes used in colored paper towels can run and stain).

Portable fans provide necessary air circulation and dehumidifiers help reduce the humidity level of the air. Wet paper and bindings will saturate the air of any room unless measures are taken to circulate fresh air and dehumidify room air.

Camera and film are needed to document the degree of damage and the recovery operation for insurance purposes. Take extensive notes as well to fully record your activities.

Protective clothing, eye goggles, gloves, and masks should be available. Masks will reduce the likelihood of breathing dirt and mold. In the event chemicals such as fungicides are used, make certain that you have appropriate protective attire.

Fumigation services or chemical supplies may be necessary to retard the growth of mold and fungus. Before applying or before allowing anyone else to apply fumigants, be confident that the applicator is knowledgeable and is using appropriate chemicals. Make an effort to be knowledgeable regarding chemicals commonly used to kill or inhibit the growth of mold or fungus. Fumigants considered safe a few years ago are now regarded with great concern.

Portable pumps and generators may be needed to remove water from a flooded area or to provide basic electrical needs for salvage operations. Be aware that most portable generators have a very limited generating capacity. You will need to determine the generating capacity needed, e.g., sufficient to operate the portable sump pump or capable of providing 600 watts of power for emergency lighting.

Other materials that should be on your list of necessary or useful equipment and supplies are:
flashlights,
library trucks,
heavy-duty extension cords,
wet-dry vacuum (carpet and padding can retain moisture and can be a breeding ground for mold),
moisture meter,
sling psychrometer (hygrometer),
two-way radios.

In the event further salvage efforts are called for at another location, you will need refrigerated trucks (except in winter, of course) to transport materials. If of sufficient value, vacuum-freeze drying may be considered. (Materials must be frozen before going into the freeze-drying chamber.)

How do you respond?

A calm and collected response to an emergency situation is largely the result of knowing what to do, either as a result of experience or planning. Since one objective of this work is to avoid experiencing a disaster, the importance of planning is obvious. One part of that planning process can be to develop a series of decision rules that will take you into the actual tasks necessary to salvage materials. For example, is the emergency localized or widespread? Is the emergency situation over or continuing? Each answer can then lead to a course of action or another question. If the emergency situation is continuing, you will, first of all, do what you can to keep damage from spreading. This may mean covering undamaged collections with plastic sheeting, for example. Whether in the planning process or as part of your response to an emergency, your priorities should be disaster (damage) avoidance, minimization, and response (salvage).

The purpose of the decision rules - really just a series of questions to direct the decision-making process - is merely to get action underway. Very often the most difficult aspect of any enterprise is simply deciding what to do. Emergencies usually do not facilitate this process. Your plan contains all those decisions you will need to make in an emergency. However, by establishing this plan you are able to make calm, collected, rational decisions based on the best available information.

Example: Heavy rains which started early in the evening caused an abnormal accumulation of water on a field behind the library. Unfortunately, a basement window was broken and the water funneled through the window into the basement. There are no drains or alarms and when the building is opened the next morning, furniture, records, and collections are floating in five feet of water. What do you do?

First of all, this is a real situation - it did happen. In addition, the files contained the results of more than 30 years worth of important research projects. Salvaging these materials was important. It was not an appropriate time to point out what might have been achieved by water alarms, functioning drains, regular inspection, and the like.

Your first question should be whether it is safe to enter the building. In particular, is the electricity disconnected? In addition, might there be structural damage which would make it dangerous to enter the building? Could a gas pipe have broken? Call the necessary services (they are on your list). Having been assured that the building is safe, you will need to pump out the water. Other questions you will be asking include:

> Has this affected any other part of the building? You may need to circulate air in the remainder of the building to reduce the humidity level. Since you are at least temporarily without electricity, you are also without air conditioning or heat. You may need a portable generator to run your fans, lights, or even your pump.

How widespread is the damage? Water may be only two feet deep in other rooms, but there may be potential damage to materials not initially soaked by the incoming water. You may be able to avoid or minimize damage in these areas by removing these items. (It is important to understand some potential problems associated with wet paper. Since paper swells as it absorbs water, it can reach a point where it is difficult to remove from shelves or from files. A full bookshelf may expand to the point of forcing out the ends of the shelving.)

How dirty is it? Is there a lot of mud or was the water relatively clean? Cleaning mud and slime from books will involve an extra procedure (see page 11).

As you look at your disaster plan in this situation, you will find your salvage priority list for the rooms affected as well as floor plans which locate these items. You will determine the extent of damage, or volume of materials damaged and, based on available facilities such as drying space, make a series of decisions. If there is not sufficient drying space for everything, you will direct that certain materials be wrapped and frozen. Assignments will be given, damp materials will be separated from wet materials, drying areas set up, and damaged materials separated into small units. Again, your disaster plan contains most of your difficult decisions. Long before the disaster occurred, decisions were made regarding who is in charge, what items would be given priority for salvage, where you would obtain needed resources, and what tasks you would undertake to salvage these materials.

Mobilizing For Salvage Operations

Attention to detail is important when responding to a disaster, and the details which need attending to should be considered in your planning. The designation of disaster response team members and alternates, ensuring that the team leader is contacted by fire department, police, or security personnel should disaster strike, and the establishment of a telephone calling tree are only the beginning steps in planning for a disaster.

If the disaster is of some magnitude, there will likely be press coverage and the magnitude of the coverage will increase with the magnitude of the disaster. Often, someone with a higher administrative position will be more effective as a public spokesperson and, as a happy circumstance, probably less effective in directing the detailed salvage operations. Make your assignments accordingly and assign responsibilities based on ensuring the most effective salvage operations.

Volunteers may be needed to help in the early salvage efforts. A public appeal for volunteers will likely receive a good response. It is important that you be ready to work with those who volunteer their time and talent. Someone must be assigned the responsibility of training volunteers, organizing them, and assigning tasks. It is imperative that appropriate supplies and safety equipment be available for their use and that they be dressed appropriately (or safely) for the job they are to do. Volunteers should wear something (badge, vest, armband) which distinguishes them from the merely curious. Volunteers and staff alike need to be provided food and drink and given regular rest breaks. Work in shifts of 8 hours to avoid problems of fatigue and do not expect the enthusiasm of either volunteers or staff to last more than 3 days. Finally, maintain a register of those who volunteer so that each can be sent a personal, written "thank you."

III. SALVAGE PROCEDURES FOR WATER-DAMAGED MATERIALS*

A number of options are available for treating water-damaged materials. The choice of treatment will depend upon the extent and type of damage incurred, and the manpower, expertise and facilities available.

Vacuum freeze drying is the safest and most successful method, although it is also the most expensive. Materials must be frozen when they are placed in a sublimation chamber. This type of chamber operates under high vacuum and high heat, and turns the ice crystals in and on the frozen materials to water vapor. The vapor is then collected on a cold panel that has been chilled to at least -200° F, so it cannot go back on the materials. If they are not frozen when they are put in the chamber, the materials will freeze on the outside and the water molecules on the inside will be forced through the frozen barrier as the vacuum is pulled. This action can cause the book or document to "explode." When the materials are removed from the chamber, they will be very dry and should acclimate for a least one month before they are opened to avoid cracking the spine and/or binding. They may be placed in a high humidity room to facilitate this process, but must be monitored closely for signs of mold. Materials so treated will not look like new, but will show signs of swelling and distortion.

Vacuum drying involves the placement of wet materials in a chamber that pulls the moisture by means of a vacuum. This method is not recommended as it is damaging to paper (especially bound paper) and photographic materials. Microwave ovens should not be used for the same reason.

Freezing wet materials will stabilize them and provide you with time to determine your course of action. Mold will not grow and further deterioration from water will not occur when materials are frozen. Books have been left in a freezer for ten years with no resultant damage. Materials that have been frozen have been successfully thawed and air-dried. Freezing will also help to eliminate smoke odor from materials. Rapid freezing is recommended to minimize damage from ice crystals (the faster the materials are frozen, the smaller the ice crystals will be). Temperatures below 15° F will freeze and dry out wet materials. If freezer space is not immediately available, and the temperature is no warmer than 15° F, place the materials in a secure area outside. Cover them with plastic if rain or snow is expected. After materials have been removed from the freezer, they should be placed in a vacuum freeze dryer or air-dried.

*By Toby Murray, University of Tulsa, "Oklahoma Chapter of the Western Conservation Congress Basic Guidelines for Disaster Planning." Used with permission.

Air-drying should be performed only in a stable environment to inhibit the growth of mold. The ideal environment for air-drying is 50-60° F and 25-35% RH. This process is not recommended for coated stock materials (see III).

The following procedures are recommended:

I. Volumes to be frozen

A. Removal

1. Clear the floors and aisles first.

2. Begin with the wettest materials. These will usually be on the lowest shelves, unless water has come in through the ceiling.

3. Ideally, dirt and mold should be removed and treated before freezing (see II.A and VI). However, time may not permit these activities. Dirty/moldy books may be frozen (mud will easily brush off when it is dry).

4. Pack materials on-site, if possible. If not possible, remove by human chain.

5. Keep accurate records of the locations from which materials are removed.

6. Pack items in the condition in which they are found. DO NOT ATTEMPT TO CLOSE OPEN VOLUMES OR OPEN CLOSED VOLUMES THAT ARE WET.

B. Packing

1. Remove volumes from shelves in order.

2. Wrap freezer paper around each volume (waxed side next to volume) and place in plastic crates spine down.

3. Pack crates one layer only, snugly enough that volumes will not slide or lean.

4. Wrap open books as found and place on top of a packed container. Do not place more than one open volume in a container. Be sure there is a freezer paper barrier between the packed volumes and the open volume to prevent staining from binding dyes.

5. If books are stuck together, do not attempt to separate them, but pack them as one volume.

C. Record-keeping

1. Label each container with your institution's name and assign it a number.

2. On a separate sheet of paper, record the box number, call numbers of the first and last volumes packed, and the total number of books in each container.

3. If the containers are sent to more than one freezer, note which container numbers are sent where.

D. Transporting

1. Materials should be placed in a freezer facility as quickly as possible to prevent the growth of mold. Care should be taken that containers do not fall over during transport, as further damage may result.

2. Refrigerated trucks may be utilized if the materials cannot be frozen within forty-eight hours.

II. Volumes to be air-dried

A. Washing procedure (to be performed off-site only)

1. Keep the book tightly closed and immerse it in the first washing tank. (Consult Peter Waters' publication for instructions.)

2. Dab the binding gently with a sponge while holding the book under water, removing as much mud as possible. Do <u>not</u> rub or use brushes and do <u>not</u> sponge the pages or edges, as these actions can force the mud into the spine or on the wet pages, causing further damage to the volume. Let the motion of the running water clean off the dirt.

3. Repeat in other washing tanks, progressing to the final rinse tank.

4. Hold the book under a gentle spray rinse.

5. Squeeze the book gently and with even pressure to remove excess water and to reshape the binding.

6. Do <u>NOT</u> wash

a. open or swollen volumes

b. vellum or parchment bindings or pages

c. leather bound volumes (full or partial bindings)

d. fragile materials

e. works of art on paper

f. water-soluble components (inks, watercolors, tempera, dyes, charcoal, etc.)

g. manuscripts

h. non-paper materials

B. Saturated volumes

1. DO NOT OPEN -- wet paper tears easily!

2. Set volumes on their heads on absorbent paper. Pages tend to droop within the binding when a volume is shelved upright, so setting it on its head will counteract this tendency. Plastic sheeting should be placed under the paper toweling or unprinted newsprint to protect table tops. Turn the volumes right side up when changing the paper beneath them. The position should be reversed each time the paper is changed and the wet paper removed from the area.

3. Covers may be opened to support the volume.

4. Aluminum foil may be placed between the cover and endleaf to prevent staining from the binding dyes.

5. When most of the water has drained, proceed as for "Damp volumes."

C. Damp volumes

1. Very carefully open the book (not more than a 30 degree angle).

2. Begin interleaving from the back and keep the volume in an upright position.

3. Place interleaving sheets at intervals of twenty-five leaves (fifty pages), unless they will distort the volume.

4. Change interleaving frequently. Do not reuse unless the sheets are being impregnated with fungicide. Ortho-Phenyl Phenol (O-PP) has been found to be less toxic than thymol and is recommended. Mix one pound of O-PP to one gallon of acetone or ethanol. (Methanol is not recommended as it will cause inks to bleed.) Safety equipment (mask, eye goggles,

and rubber gloves) should be worn when preparing and using this solution.

5. Continue to change the paper underneath and remove from the area.

D. Slightly damp volumes/Volumes with only wet edges

1. Stand volume on its head and fan open slightly. Paperback books may support each other with a barrier between them or they may be wedged with styrofoam pieces. Position volumes in the path of circulating air.

2. When almost dry, lay the volumes flat and place weights (not other drying books) on them to minimize distortion. DO NOT STACK WET VOLUMES.

3. Lightweight volumes (less than six pounds) may be hung on a line to dry.

a. Use monofilament nylon, not more than 1/32" diameter, not more than five or six feet long, and spaced approximately one-half inch apart.

b. Do not line-dry a saturated volume as the monofilament will cut through the wet paper.

III. Volumes with coated stock paper

Do not attempt to air-dry wet books with coated stock paper as the pages will permanently bond together. Almost all attempts to separate stuck pages by rewetting them have failed. The only chance of saving such materials is to interleave and air-dry them immediately, or to freeze them while wet and then vacuum freeze dry them.

A. Handle with care, as the print will slide off the wet page.

B. If not frozen immediately, keep them submerged until they can be separated (see IV.B). Interleave every page and air-dry.

IV. Documents/Unbound materials

A. Freeze as found

1. Do not remove from document cases or folders.

2. Do not turn file cabinets or document cases upside down to empty or drain.

B. Separation of wet sheets

1. Place a sheet of polyester film on top of a stack of wet, unbound papers.

2. Rub gently with a bone folder -- surface friction will cause the wet paper to adhere to the film.

3. Peel back the top sheet and place it on top of a piece of polyester web.

4. Remove the polyester film.

5. Place another piece of polyester web on top of the wet sheet.

6. Repeat the entire process, separating the wet sheets one at a time and interleaving them with polyester web. (Materials may be frozen at this stage.)

7. Air-dry the sheets (supported by the polyester web) by placing them on absorbent paper on tables or on closely spaced monofilament lines. Air in the room should be kept circulating, but fans should <u>not</u> blow directly on the materials.

8. The papers may be flattened when they are almost dry by placing them between two sheets of blotting paper (to remove excess moisture) and applying even pressure with weights.

V. Non-book materials

A. Photographic materials (prints, negatives, slides, film)

Do not expect to salvage color photographs, as the colored layers will separate and the dyes will fade quickly. However, if you wish to attempt to salvage color photographs, freeze them immediately or transport them (see 2 below) to a professional photographic laboratory.

Photographic materials should not be allowed to dry out after they become wet as they will stick to their envelopes or to each other. Any attempt to separate them after they have dried together will result in damage to the emulsion or the image. Remove the materials from their protective enclosures and wash off any mud or dirt under cold, clean running water.

The following options are available for salvaging photographic materials:

1. Air-dry either flat or on lines of monofilament (plastic spring-type clothespins may be used to hang them on the lines).

2. If there are too many to air-dry, they may be stored in cold water (65° F or below -- cold helps to preserve the emulsion). Ice may be added to the water, but do <u>not</u> add dry ice or allow the materials to remain under water longer than three days. Formaldehyde may be added to the water (fifteen milliliters to one liter) to help prevent the gelatin from swelling and softening. Black and white film could last three days in this solution before the emulsion begins to separate; color film could last forty-eight hours. Transport them (in sealed polyethylene bags inside plastic garbage pails) to a professional laboratory within twenty-four hours, if possible.

3. If time does not permit air-drying, the materials may be frozen as in I above. As the emulsion may be damaged by the formation of ice crystals, freezing as quickly as possible is recommended (smaller ice crystals will cause less damage). Negatives should be separated before freezing, as they can stick together after thawing and drying.

4. The Eastman Kodak Company provides free emergency service for cleaning and drying its own or unknown brands of black-and-white film. They will work on other brands of film for cost.

B. Microforms

1. Silver halide microfilm

   a. Keep under water (see V.A.2).

   b. Send to Kodak or microprocessing laboratory.

2. Vesicular and diazo microfilm

   a. Wash off mud or dirt under cold, clean running water.

   b. Air-dry or dry with cheesecloth.

3. Microfiche

   a. Treat the same as microfilm.

   b. Kodak will not treat microfiche, so send them to a professional microprocessing laboratory.

C. Tapes (audio, video, computer) and floppy disks

Water is especially damaging to magnetic tapes and disks. The longer these materials have been wet, the greater the damage will be. Generally, magnetic media should be considered unrecoverable. For this reason it is important to back up magnetic media, such as computer tapes and disks, and to store the back up in a separate location. Do not attempt to play any damaged tapes, as they can damage the equipment on which they are being played. Success has been reported in the salvage of floppy diskettes by removing them from their jackets, carefully cleaning the diskettes in multiple baths of distilled water and, after drying, inserting into a new empty jacket. The following procedures are recommended if you wish to attempt to salvage audio tapes:

1. Break open the cassettes.

2. Wash in clean or distilled water.

3. Air-dry or dry with cheesecloth.

4. Wind against a felt pad to remove excess water.

D. Sound recordings (disks)

Clean water probably will not damage sound recordings, but flood water carries silt, which will scratch a disk. Disks should be washed and dried with cheesecloth or a soft, lint-free cloth. Record jackets or paper protective sleeves should be discarded as they can trap moisture and may develop mold. The record jacket may be photocopied to preserve the information on it.

VI. Mold

Mold and mildew are interchangeable terms for fungi. They can never be killed and can remain dormant for many years. Spores are always present in the air and will grow when the environment is warm and humid. Freezing will inhibit the growth of mold and is recommended if time does not permit immediate treatment.

A. Mold can develop within 48-72 hours in an environment where the temperature is over 75° F and the relative humidity is over 60%.

B. Separate the affected materials to prevent spreading.

C. If the materials are wet and mold is beginning to develop, interleave the volumes with papers impregnated with a fungicide (see II.C.4).

D. Keep the air circulating in the room.

E. Mold is easier to remove when it is dry. Vacuum or brush it off and remove the spores from the area.

F. Fungicidal fogging should be done only by a professional chemist or conservator. Materials should be removed from plastic milk crates, as the plastic will absorb the fumigants.

VII. Don't just do something -- stand there!

DO NOT, UNDER ANY CIRCUMSTANCES,

... enter an area until it has been declared safe to do so.

... attempt to open a wet book (one tear costs at least one dollar to mend!).

... attempt to close an open book that has swollen.

... use mechanical presses on wet materials.

... attempt to separate books that are stuck together.

... write on wet paper.

... use bleaches, detergents, water-soluble fungicides, staples, paper clips, adhesive tapes, or adhesives of any kind on wet materials.

... use colored paper of any kind during salvage and recovery operations.

... pack newly-dried materials in boxes or leave unattended for more than two days.

IV. SUGGESTED PLAN OUTLINE

DISASTER PREPAREDNESS PLAN

PURPOSE: This plan outlines procedures and assigns duties relating to preventing, minimizing, and responding to emergencies which threaten people and materials.

PERSONNEL: There is hereby established an Emergency Preparedness Team responsible for identifying, correcting, and monitoring hazardous conditions within the ______________ system and for responding to disasters which may occur. Team members are responsible for specific areas or activities both for purposes of disaster prevention and for response to an emergency.

Team Member/ Alternates		Home Telephone	Responsibilities
Team Leader	______________	______________	Overall management of operation; co-ordination with administrative offices; budget allocation for wages, supplies, transportation, and services; public relations.
Alternate	______________	______________	
Member	______________	______________	Assemble and co-ordinate work crews; control work and materials flow.
Alternate	______________	______________	
Member	______________	______________	Record/inventory control of damaged materials.
Alternate	______________	______________	
Member	______________	______________	Damage/salvage assessment; co-ordinate recovery effort, train work crews.
Alternate	______________	______________	
Member	______________	______________	Assemble supplies and equipment, provide food for work crews, photograph damage and recovery operation.
Alternate	______________	______________	

OTHER SERVICES NEEDED:

Name of Service	Telephone	Name of Person or Company
Fire Department	________	____________________
Police or Sheriff	________	____________________
Ambulance	________	____________________
Disaster Emergency Services	224-3300	____________________
Electric Company	________	____________________
Water Company	________	____________________
Gas Company	________	____________________
Telephone Company	________	____________________
Insurance Company	________	____________________
Extra security personnel	________	____________________
Janitorial service	________	____________________
Volunteer organizations (to assist in salvage and clean-up)	________	____________________
Electrician	________	____________________
Plumber	________	____________________
Locksmith	________	____________________
Exterminator	________	____________________
Legal Advisor	________	____________________
Carpenter	________	____________________
Mycologist	________	____________________
Chemist	________	____________________
____________________	________	____________________
____________________	________	____________________

FLOOR PLANS:

Attached as an appendix to this plan should be a set or series of floor plans which locate the items enumerated below. One set of floor plans can be used and the various items color-coded. The complexity of the floor plans depends in part on the complexity of the structure in question. It is important to note that floor plans do not take the place of tours which point out to all staff the location of these materials. In all cases, however, the following items should be identified.

Utilities:

1. Main electrical cut-off.
2. Main gas shut-off.
3. Main water shut-off.
4. Sprinkler system shut-off (may be separate from water shut-off).

Exits and evacuation routes. In the case of building evacuation, there should be agreed-upon responsibilities, established routes and alternatives for evacuating each area, and an agreed-upon meeting place outside of the building so that all occupants of the building are accounted for.

On-site emergency supplies and equipment, including
fire extinguishers and alarms,
smoke and water detectors and alarms,
plastic sheeting stored with scissors and tape,
first aid kit,
portable pump, and
other supplies and equipment which are part of your list.

Vital records and key collections. The priorities for saving both records and collections should be established for each area of the building (see next section) since damage may be confined to certain areas or there may be an opportunity to access one part of the building before another.

PRIORITIES:

This section should contain a listing of all supplies, equipment, furnishings (e.g., original art), materials, both collections and library records, which will be given priority for salvage in the event of a disaster. As in other areas of the plan, there is no need for long narrative or a justification for these decisions. That has been resolved in the planning process. This plan is an action document and the people using it should be familiar with its purposes. Your priorities will consist of two lists. The first is a list of **overall priorities**, based on the assumption that all areas of the building and all materials have suffered or have the potential of suffering the same fate. The second is a list of **priorities by area**, section, or room. In the case of a larger institution, you may be organized as several teams, each responsible for a given section or functional area of the building.

PROCEDURES:

This section spells out who to contact and the procedures for initiating action. For example, a telephone tree should be established. The team leader may call a second team member and assign responsibility for contacting other team members. In a larger organization, the team leader may contact committee or group leaders who are then responsible for assembling their teams. Seemingly simple matters should be addressed. Should team members automatically assemble at a predetermined location upon hearing of an emergency or await contact by the designated team member?

This section also provides those decision rules which facilitate action. What items must be checked to determine that the building is safe to enter? Can the salvage effort be handled without outside assistance? Will washing be necessary? The answer to each question will, in most instances, establish a procedure and define responsibility (e.g., if washing of books is necessary, the washing procedure described in Waters, Procedures for Salvage... will be followed, the work will be conducted at A or alternate site B, C will be in charge, assisted by D, E, and F).

Finally, or perhaps firstly, this section should define those routine maintenance procedures dealing with disaster prevention. For example, "staff member A, or in A's absence, staff member B, will daily check the following items: (1) all materials of the floor, (2) aisles and work areas free of clutter and debris," and so on. Not the least of these procedures is an annual review of the disaster plan. Sources may have changed and new circumstances introduced. New ideas may have been generated, and the regular inspections may have yielded additional insight into potential problem areas. In addition, regular review will make staff better equipped to handle whatever situation might arise. This review should include touring of the building by all staff to locate extinguishers, alarms, and other equipment and supplies. The review will benefit from following other annual procedures, such as fire drills, fire department inspection, and building inspection.

EMERGENCY EQUIPMENT AND SUPPLIES:

While some emergency supplies and equipment should be on hand at all times, it would be impossible to stock such items in sufficient quantities to meet all contingencies. It is necessary, however, to know sources of supply where items can be purchased, borrowed, or rented. In some cases it is a good idea to have contingency suppliers as well since, in a wide-scale, major disaster, your sources may not be available because they have their own damages to deal with or because they are assisting someone else. Do not overlook businesses or other organizations who might be willing and able to loan necessary resources. It will be useful to discuss your plans with most of your suppliers, including rental firms, so that precious time is not wasted obtaining authorizations when an emergency arises. Explain your needs and purpose to your sources of supplies and contact them on a regular basis to determine whether they are still available and to remind them of their commitment.

Item	Supplier and name of contact	Telephone
Drying space		
Plastic garbage cans		
Plastic crates or card-board boxes		
Freezer space		
Plastic trash bags*		
Freezer or Wax paper*		
Plastic sheeting (rolls)*		
Unprinted newsprint		
Paper towels (plain white)*		
Portable fans		
Portable dehumidifiers		
Camera/film*		
Rubber gloves*		
Protective masks*		

Fungicides (OPP or Thymol crystals & alcohol		
Portable sump pump		
Portable generator		
Flashlights*		
Library trucks		
Heavy-duty Extension cords*		
Wet-dry vacuum		
Moisture meter		
Sling psychrometer (hygrometer)*		
Two-way radios		
Refrigerator trucks		
Water hoses		
Pails, mops, sponges*		
Brooms*		
Nylon Monofilament		
Forklift and pallets		

* Indicates items which should be on hand in at least limited quantities.

NOTES ON SOURCES OF SUPPLIES, EQUIPMENT, AND SERVICES:

The availability of supplies, equipment, and services will vary significantly throughout the state. In some cases it will be more important to be able to locate a supplier nearby. In all cases it is important to anticipate what will be needed to obtain the needed supplies, equipment, or services. Most important may be the authority to commit funds to purchase or rent what is needed.

A large amount of drying space may be required. Look to such places as gymnasiums, or auditoriums, or warehouses which are not only spacious but also capable of being ventilated easily to avoid buildup of humidity. Locker plants, warehouses, and large groceries may be able to provide temporary freezer space, but be aware of possible health and sanitation requirements which might prevent the storage of water-damaged books with frozen food.

Garbage cans, plastic trash bags, freezer paper, plastic sheeting, paper towels, film, rubber gloves, protective masks, flashlights, heavy-duty extension cords, water hoses, pails, mops, sponges, brooms, and nylon monofilament (used for drip-drying) are all fairly easily obtainable from hardware stores, large discount stores, and from some drug and food stores. Key considerations are quantities available and authorization to purchase the materials available.

Forklifts and pallets (used to load large quantities of heavy wet volumes onto trucks), fans, dehumidifiers, sump pumps, generators, radios, and refrigerator trucks are all items which can usually be rented or borrowed. Most of the state's larger cities have one or more equipment rental firms which can supply a number of these items. An important consideration is that in the event of a wide-spread emergency many of the items (e.g., generators and sump pumps) may be in heavy demand. Be able to act quickly to obtain what is needed.

Unprinted newsprint may be available from a local newspaper or paper supplier. Cardboard boxes (standard records boxes are 12x15x10 inches) may be more available (and preferable to) plastic crates for packing out. Look to box companies or moving companies as possible sources of supply. Plastic milk crates may be available from a local dairy. Library trucks may not be readily available in any quantity. Consider substitutes such as grocery shopping carts or wheelbarrows.

In the event of a disaster you may want or need to turn to a professional salvage expert or you may require vacuum freeze drying services. There are a number of facilities and providers of services available. Document Reprocessors offers all restoration services from boxing and removing, drying and cleaning, to reshelving and refiling for all types of water damage from fire to flood. They have portable equipment and offer on-site services. Contact:

Document Reprocessors
41 Sutter Street, Suite 1120
San Francisco, CA 94104
ATTN: Eric G. Lundquist
Telephone: 1-800-4-DRYING

McDonnell Douglas in St. Louis will provide vacuum freeze drying services. For information and current costs, contact:

Ben Bull, Document Reclamation Service
McDonnell Aircraft Company
Department 256, Building 102, Post L140
Post Office Box 516
St. Louis, MO 63166
Telephone: 314-232-5076

Other companies and organizations offering professional services to assist in disaster recovery include:

Blackmon-Mooring-Steamatic Catastrophic, Inc. (BMS Cat)
One Summit Ave., Suite 202
Fort Worth, TX 76102
Telephone: 1-800-433-2940
(Offers an extensive array of services, including drying, fumigation, and cleanup of building interiors and contents.)

Northeast Document Conservation Center
Abbott Hall, 24 School Street
Andover, MA 01810
Telephone: 617-470-1010
(Offers disaster consulting services.)

Kodak Microfilm Division
Rochester, NY
Telephone: 716-724-4876
(Salvage of microfilm.)

Kodak Processing Division
Chicago, IL
Telephone: 312-635-5956 or 5957
(Emergency salvage advice.)

DISTRIBUTION AND LOCATION:

Copies of this plan have been given to the following individuals (Team members should receive two copies and keep one at home and one in their office):

In addition, copies of this plan can be found in the following locations:

1. In house:

2. Off-site:

This plan was last reviewed and updated on ____________________.

APPENDIX A

READINESS CHECKLIST

	Activity	Frequency of Activity	Date Completed or checked
1.	Windows, skylights in good repair	semi-annual	
2.	Door and window locks operable and secure and keys accounted for		
3.	Roof inspected and secure		
4.	Gutters/downspouts clear and operating properly	semi-annual	
5.	Aisles, work areas free of clutter and debris	daily	
6.	Electrical equipment in supervised area away from collections		
7.	Smoke alarms operable and properly placed	monthly	
8.	Water detectors operable	monthly	
9.	All materials stored at least 3 inches off the floor		
10.	Sprinkler system or other fire suppression systems operable		
11.	Regular inspection by local fire department	annual	
12.	Training in use of fire extinguishers by local fire department		
13.	Furnace/air conditioner checked/ serviced	annual	
14.	Electrical system inspected		
15.	Plumbing system inspected		
16.	Fire extinguishers updated and operable		

Readiness Checklist Continued

17.	Insurance coverage needs analyzed and updated	annual	
18.	Fire doors ready for emergency use		
19.	All staff knowledgeable regarding:		
	a. location and use of fire extinguishers and other equipment	annual*	
	b. emergency shelter procedure	"	
	c. evacuation procedure	"	
	d. disaster preparedness plan	"	
20.	Team meeting and review of disaster plan	annual*	
21.	Fire drill	annual*	
22.	Flashlights operable	monthly	
23.	Emergency numbers posted by every telephone	daily (semi-annual update)	
24.	Portable radio operable	monthly	
25.	First aid kit complete	monthly	
26.	Disaster preparedness plan reviewed and updated	annual	
27.	Staff trained in CPR recertified	annual	

*Minimum frequency

OCCIDENTAL COLLEGE LIBRARY

EARTHQUAKE PREPAREDNESS AND SURVIVAL PLANS

Occidental College

TABLE OF CONTENTS

A WORD FROM THE COMMITTEE:

Emergency readiness means that you are prepared to react promptly to save lives and protect property. You are only prepared through careful planning and preparations BEFORE there is an emergency.

Our purpose has been to prepare a procedural guide detailing what is to be done at the College during and after an earthquake of significant magnitude.

The College plan will not succeed unless every employee has made survival plans on a personal level which takes into account their home, their families (including pets) and themselves. You will be given a personal copy of Libby Lafferty's Earthquake Preparedness to help you prepare at the home front.

Laura Serafini, Chair
Kim Ellis
Kim Esser
Alfred Gonsalves

Occidental College

INTRODUCTION:

Most of the information in this manual comes from the 1986 report of the Occidental College *ad hoc* Earthquake Preparedness Committee. The results of that committee's research is summarized in the following points:

1. It is better to be over rather than underprepared.
   The College should be able to respond to a major earthquake disaster which could involve widespread injury to people and damage to structures and property.

2. There will be a probable time period of 72 hours of self-sufficiency before receiving help from other community services.

3. What to expect during an earthquake:

   - Everything shakes and rattles

   - There will be a lot of noise

   - Things will fall and break (such as ceiling tiles, bookcases, file cabinets, desks, and other furniture).

   - The motion will be severe - if you are standing, you may be thrown to the ground.

   - Most things will stop working (lights, telephones, computers, elevators, heat and air-conditioning).

   - Most windows will probably break, shattering glass into and around buildings and allowing strong drafts. There will be a big and dangerous mess.

   - Fires started by electrical short-circuits may well be fed by broken natural gas lines. Because water lines might be broken, these fires could possibly burn out of control.

   - Buildings may collapse totally or partially. There may be many injured and some dead.

4. Overview of the Oxy Campus Emergency Action Plan

A. WHO IS IN CHARGE?

EMERGENCY COORDINATORS

Security, Dean of Students, VP for Business & Finance, Dean of Faculty and others as designated by the President. These persons will be in charge of the overall emergency operation under the direction of the ranking officer present.

|

INCIDENT COMMANDER: HEAD OF SECURITY

The incident commander will be constantly receiving information from other task force members, security in the field, outside sources, etc., in order to assess the injuries and damage and coordinate rescue operations and other emergency services.

|

BUILDING MONITORS

Designated administrators, faculty and staff will be in charge of each building on campus. It is the responsibility of each building monitor to have an up-to-date list of all building occupants and who are first aid certified. All building monitors must take an immediate head count, determine who is missing, who is injured, and who is able to help with rescue operations.

|

FLOOR MONITORS

Floor Monitors will be responsible for overseeing a designated floor. If it is necessary to evacuate any floor, Floor Monitors will determine the location and status of any hazards and will direct building occupants to the assembly area, indicating which stairwells to use. Floor Monitors should report back to the Building Monitors when the location or relocation of employees is complete, and the damage and hazards are determined.

|

DEPARTMENT HEADS

Within departments, Department Heads (or designated persons in their absence) should take charge of their areas. They will account for their personnel, check for injuries and treat as best as possible. Department Heads will also be responsible for locating secondary hazards (such as fires, toxic spills, etc.), clearing the immediate area of personnel and eliminating the hazards if it is safe to do so. If personnel must be evacuated, the Department Head will follow procedures indicated by the Floor Monitor or Building Monitor.

B. WHERE IS THE CENTER OF OPERATION? WHERE ARE THE GATHERING AREAS?

COMMAND AREA - CENTER OF OPERATION:

Security will be the Command Center of coordination of both rescue efforts and emergency actions and will be moved to the Plant Offices if the size of the earthquake requires more operating space, or if the building (Emmons) is seriously damaged.

CENTRAL ASSEMBLY AREA:

Pattersson Field is designated as the major assembly area in the event of major damage to facilities (Anderson Field is an additional area for upper campus if necessary).

SATELLITE ASSEMBLY AREAS:

Every building will be assigned to a satellite assembly area for initial head counts, gathering of information, damage assessments, etc.

FOOD:

Oxy Food Services will be prepared to set up alternative dining facilities and able to serve 10,000 meals.

Occidental College

HOW TO PREPARE:

1. Be familiar with the Campus Emergency Action plan.
   Know who is the Building Monitor and who are the Floor Monitors.

2. Be familiar with the Library's floor plans.

3. Know where all the stairs and exits are.

4. Know where all the fire extinguishers are and how to use them.

5. Know where the Library's emergency supplies are kept.

6. Maintain a personal at-work survival kit. Include the following items:
   - Water
   - Emergency food rations
   - First aid kit and critical medication
   - Battery radio
   - Flashlight with batteries or lightsticks
   - Comfortable shoes and extra clothing
   - Blanket
   - Money for telephone
   - Phone number of out of state contact
   - Ziplock bags, toilet tissue
   - Book to read, pack of cards, etc.

7. Make sure your family has an operational survival plan.

WHAT TO DO DURING THE SHAKING:

1. IF YOU ARE INSIDE THE LIBRARY...

   - DO NOT PANIC

   - DO NOT RUSH OUTSIDE

   - DO NOT ATTEMPT TO USE THE ELEVATORS

   - REMAIN CALM -- *THE SHAKING WILL EVENTUALLY STOP*

   - Get under your desk or other sturdy furniture and hold on. If you are not near any suitable furniture, move to a corner or solid wall and crouch down (make yourself as small as possible) to protect your head and neck with whatever is available such as a book, notebook, briefcase, large purse, suit coat, etc. Much of the Library has fake drop-ceiling tiles that are easily shaken loose by quakes, so protecting your head with something is a must.

   - Stay near the center of the building.

   - Stay away from glass windows, skylights, and doors.

   - If you stand in a doorway, take precautions so that you are not beaten by the door.

   - Stay away from shelves and bookcases that might fall over.

   - Stay clear of heavy furniture and equipment that might be thrown at you.

2. IF YOU ARE OUTSIDE...

   - REMAIN CALM -- *THE SHAKING WILL EVENTUALLY STOP*

   - Get into an open area, away from buildings and utility wires.

WHAT TO DO AFTER THE SHAKING:

1. GENERAL

- **DON'T PANIC.** Stop and take time to think.

- **DO NOT LEAVE THE CAMPUS**

- Do not light matches, cigarettes, or turn on lights or machines.

- Do not use the elevators.

- Do not use the telephone. FYI: Primary lines will be the first to come back on if telephone service is interrupted. (Primary lines are pay phones and out of state lines. This is why an out of state contact for all the members of your family to check in with is a good idea.)

- Take the time to change into the shoes in your at-work survival kit.

- Report to your building monitor (see section #2).

2. THE EMERGENCY ACTION PLAN

When it is safe, leave the building and report to the Library's assembly area to be accounted for. The assembly area assigned to the library is located:

____

The Building Monitor will be there to account for all persons in the Library and mobilize rescue teams and direct the efforts in conjunction with the Campus Emergency Task Forces.

WHAT IF...

exits are blocked?... The Floor Monitor will investigate all exit hazards and help will be on its way.

your are injured and need help?... Your department head will assess your injuries and report them to the Building Monitor and help will be on its way.

you know there are patrons that are trapped?... Report this to the Floor Monitor or the Building Monitor and help will be on its way.

WHAT IF... (continued)

you saw a broken water pipe?... your saw shorting electrical circuits?... Report this to the Floor Monitor or the Building Monitor.

you saw a fire start?... Decide if you can get to the nearest fire extinguisher and suppress the flames. Get the information to the Floor Monitor or the Building Monitor.

All injury and hazard information needs to be communicated to the Building monitor at the Library assembly area. On the judgement and direction of the Building Monitor, first aid and rescue help will be sent in teams of at least two persons.

3. CAUTIONS AND REMINDERS

- Do not attempt to move seriously injured persons unless they are in immediate danger of further injury.

- If evacuated upon order of the Building Monitor, take your personal belongings and your at-work survival kit. Stand by to help bring out the Library emergency supplies.

- Be prepared for aftershocks.

- Be part of the solution, not part of the problem. (Don't become a victim because of bad judgement)

- Always work in pairs.

- Wear protective equipment (gloves, hats, goggles).

- Everyone will experience some degree of emotional trauma. Know your stress level. Do not participate in any rescue efforts unless you feel up to it. Don't push yourself beyond the point which you are able to help.

- FYI: The "Good Samaritan" law from the California Civil Code, Chapter 9, Section 1799.102, says that if you offer help, not for compensation, at the scene of a disaster (emergency), you shall not be liable for civil damages resulting from any act or omission.

Occidental College

PERSONNEL POLICY:

During working hours, employees will be expected to remain on campus until notified by the Emergency Task Force that it is safe to travel. Where rescue work is required, it is hope that volunteers will remain on campus and assist where needed.

After working hours, employees should attempt to call to see if their services are needed. Those employees who live in the immediate area are requested to come to the College as soon as practical to determine if their help is needed.

Two of the biggest questions in the event of a major earthquake will be "can we go home?" and "will we be paid for our time?"

The first question should be answered in the affirmative as soon as campus emergency coordinators deem it safe to allow employees to travel (whether by car or on foot) for any who wish to leave to check on children or other dependents, or who have other significant personal reasons for leaving.
However, it should by clear that department heads should not release employees until such safe travel conditions have been announced by those in charge, probably through the communication channels of Building Monitors.

The second question, "will I be paid?", will require a policy decision. The Personnel Director's recommendation would be along the following lines. The College should designate a duration of time through which hourly employees will be paid for their regularly scheduled work hours if they are actively at work, (or on approved paid sick leave or vacation), and leave work with the approval of the department head at the time of an earthquake that results in employees being sent home. Given the frequent reference to a 72 hour (3 day) period of emergency action, that paid status duration might be for the scheduled worked hours in the three calendar days immediately following the earthquake for all employees for whom work is not available and/or who are not able to return to campus because of family crises or related emergencies. After that time, if certain employees are still not back on the job, they would be place on "leave without pay" status until such time as they return to active work, unless they choose to use accumulated vacation time to remain on pay status, or would otherwise qualify for paid sick leave benefits.

ABOUT LIABILITY FOR INJURIES TO EMPLOYEES:
The College has made inquiries through their Workers Compensation carrier as to the extent of College liability under that plan for employee injuries incurred at work during an earthquake. The reply to their inquiries was that this is an area that is essentially "untested", but that the insurance company would deny benefits and fight any such claims. Needless to say, that position would not constitute a final determination on such matters, and there would by other legal and administrative law avenues open to employees who wished to claim damages if injured.

APPENDIX

Occidental College

EARTHQUAKE PREPAREDNESS SUPPLIES INVENTORY

NAME Laura Serafini DEPARTMENT Library

ITEMS	QUANTITY - 4 kits
First Aid Kit	1 - 1 - 1 - 1
Flashlight	1 - 1 - 1 - 1
Batteries	2 - 2 - 2 - 2
Sanitation bags (plastic)	7 - 7 - 6 - 6
Ace bandage 3"	1 - 1 - 1 - 1
Shock blanket	1 - 1 - 1 - 1
Alcohol wipes	10 -10 -10 -10
Antiseptic wipes	10 -10 -10 -10
Tylenol packages	5 - 5 - 5 - 5
Water (2 x 2.5 gal. bottles/box)	25 gallons

Location of kits: 2 kits are located in the Library out-going mailroom in a cupboard labeled "emergency supplies 2 kits are located in the Staff Room (3rd fl. East in a kitchen cupboard labeled "emergency supplies"

Location of water: 15 gal are in the out-going mailroom cupboard
10 gal are in the Staff room kitchen cupboard

Comments. I think we need to reconsider storing emergency supplies on the 3rd floor of the East wing.

BS:cc:kitinvnt

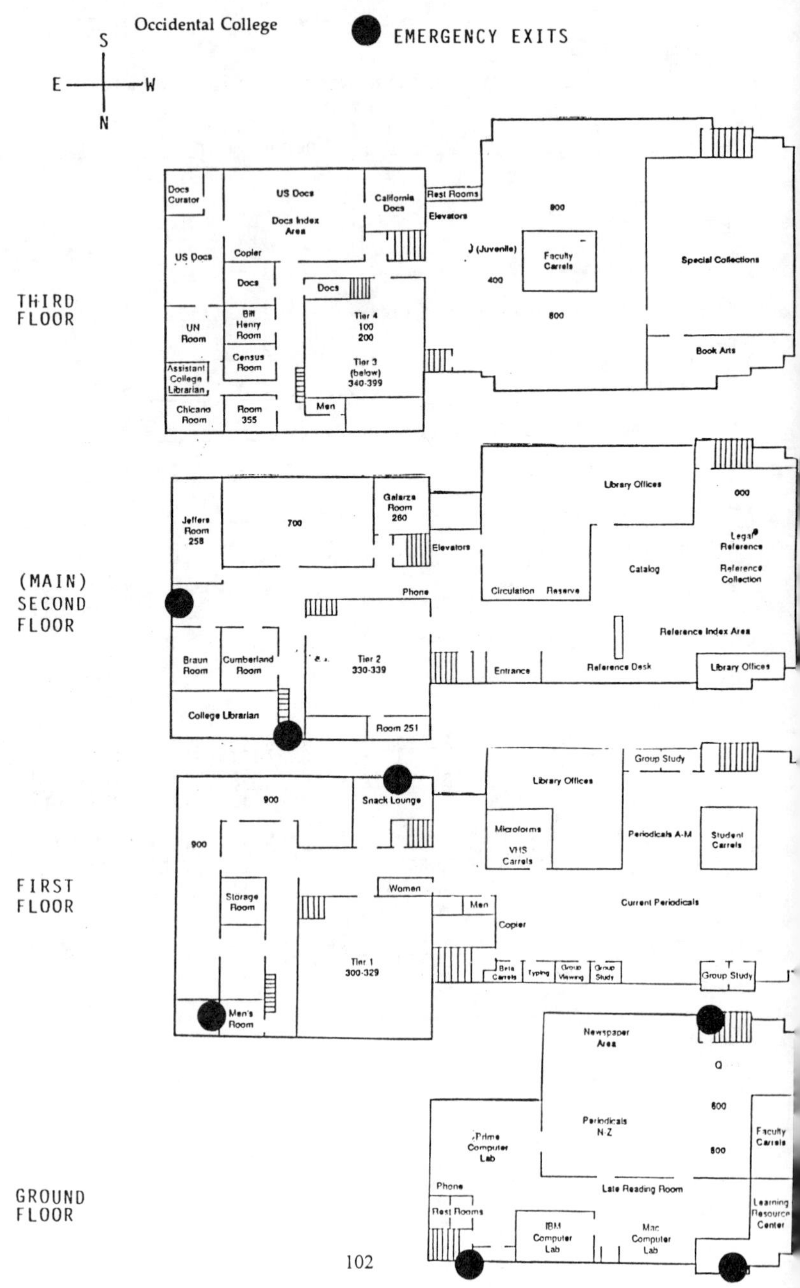

Occidental College
EMERGENCY EXITS
S
E
W
N
THIRD FLOOR
Docs Curator
US Docs
Docs Index Area
California Docs
Rest Rooms
Elevators
900
J (Juvenile)
Faculty Carrels
400
800
Special Collections
Book Arts
US Docs
Copier
Docs
Docs
Bill Henry Room
Tier 4 100 200
Tier 3 (below) 340-399
UN Room
Census Room
Assistant College Librarian
Chicano Room
Room 355
Men
(MAIN) SECOND FLOOR
Jeffers Room 258
700
Galarza Room 260
Elevators
Library Offices
000
Legal Reference
Reference Collection
Catalog
Circulation
Reserve
Phone
Reference Index Area
Braun Room
Cumberland Room
Tier 2 330-339
Entrance
Reference Desk
Library Offices
College Librarian
Room 251
FIRST FLOOR
900
Snack Lounge
Library Offices
Group Study
900
Microforms
VHS Carrels
Periodicals A-M
Student Carrels
Storage Room
Women
Men
Current Periodicals
Copier
Tier 1 300-329
Group Study
Men's Room
GROUND FLOOR
Newspaper Area
Q
600
Periodicals N-Z
Faculty Carrels
Prime Computer Lab
800
Phone
Late Reading Room
Rest Rooms
Learning Resource Center
IBM Computer Lab
Mac Computer Lab

Occidental College

FIRE EXTINGUISHERS/HOSES IN THE LIBRARY

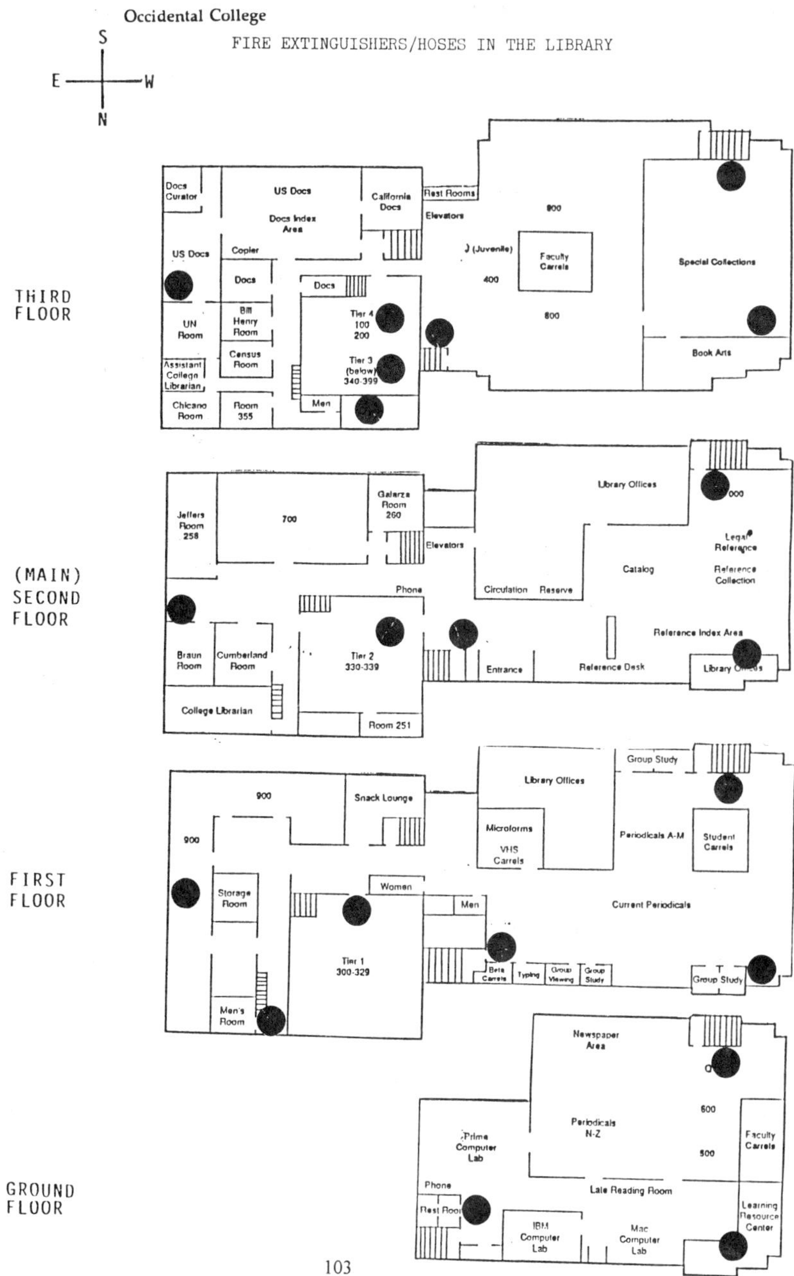

Occidental College

BEFORE AN EARTHQUAKE . . .

If you would like to test the operation of your main gas shut-off valve, the Southern California Gas Company suggests you follow the instructions below.

— FOLLOW THESE 6 STEPS —

1. Locate and identify your gas meter and main shut-off valve with those persons you believe could and should know how to shut off the gas, if necessary, after an earthquake (see checklist on back).

2. Use the illustrations of gas meters and main shut-off valves below to help identify yours.

3. Using a 12″ adjustable, or other appropriate wrench on the main shut-off valve, turn the valve no more than 1/8th turn either left or right from its vertical position and back again. This movement may at first be difficult.

= gas ON   or = 1/8 TURN

4. CAUTION: *BE CAREFUL NOT TO TURN THE MAIN SHUT-OFF VALVE MORE THAN 1/8 TURN TO THE LEFT OR RIGHT!*

5. Check your pilot lights and/or gas appliances in the building to see if they are still operating. If you have accidentally shut your main gas valve off, and you are familiar with the methods for safely relighting your appliances, slowly turn the main gas valve back on and light the pilots. If you need assistance in lighting your pilots, turn the main gas valve off and call the Gas Co. to restore service to your building.

= gas ON   = gas OFF

6. If you find that your main shut-off valve is too difficult to turn or you are unable to turn it at all, call the Gas Co. and request they come out to adjust or replace it for you.

TYPICAL GAS METER INSTALLATION

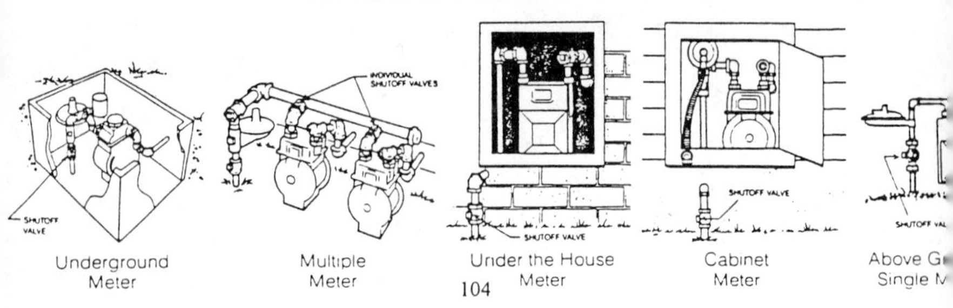

Underground Meter | Multiple Meter | Under the House Meter | Cabinet Meter | Above G Single M

AFTER AN EARTHQUAKE . .

WHEN SHOULD YOU TURN OFF YOUR MAIN GAS VALVE ???

The Los Angeles City Fire Department and the Southern California Gas Company recommend the use of this (✓) list tc help you determine when you should shut off your building's main gas valve after an earthquake occurs.

TURN OFF YOUR METER'S SHUT-OFF VALVE . .

( ) . . . ***IF*** you smell, hear or even suspect gas is escaping in your damaged, or undamaged, building(s).

( ) . . . ***IF*** your gas water heater or any other gas appliance has been knocked over and/or pulled free from its wall connection.

( ) . . . ***IF*** your building has suffered extensive damage, such as large cracks in the exterior walls or in the concrete slab floors, etc., *AND* you suspect the gas lines or appliances have been damaged.

'ARNING: It is very dangerous and therefore not recommended that yo go searching for gas leaks inside any damaged building.

BE AWARE: After an earthquake, aftershocks will continue to occur, possibly causing additional damage (or even first damage) to your building(s), for several weeks after the original event.

REMEMBER: Once you have turned off your gas service, for your safety, *DO NOT TURN IT BACK ON !* If you turn your gas off, or need other service, call the Gas Company as soon as possible.

PLEASE BE PATIENT. Earthquakes have been known to disrupt gas service for day(s) at a time. Your Gas Company will restore service to your building as soon as conditions permit. You may also contact a qualified licensed plumber to have your piping checked and gas service restored.

Occidental College

G FOR THE QUAKE

Risk

RCHANGES AND BRIDGES

AL SEIB / Los Angeles Times

s to get heavy at interchange of Hollywood and Pasadena freeways.

Caltrans' List of 44 Troublespot

These are the bridges in the Los Angeles County area that have designated by the California Department of Transportation as most lik sustain damage in an earthquake. They have been given top priorit retrofitting program designed to strengthen the ability of their colum withstand severe groundshaking. The risk rating the department has as to each bridge is based on a scale of 0.00 to 1.00, with 0.00 the least vuln and 1.00 the most vulnerable. The list represents only single column brid program to retrofit multicolumn bridges is expected to begin soon.

FREEWAY	ESTIMATED COST TO REPAIR
2 (Glendale)—crossover at I-5	$1,840,000
2 (Glendale)—westbound interchange to eastbound 134	$370,000
5 (Golden State)—crossover at Riverside Drive.	$300,000
5 (Golden State)—Griffith Park on-ramp, overcrossing at I-5	$190,000
5 (Golden State)—Griffith Park off-ramp, overcrossing at I-5	$230,000
10 (San Bernardino)—pedestrian overcrossing near Evergreen Avenue	$130,000
10 (San Bernardino)—pedestrian overcrossing near Marguerita Avenue	$190,000
10 (Santa Monica)—westbound interchange to southbound 101	$400,000
10 (San Bernardino)—pedestrian overcrossing near City Terrace Drive	$270,000
10 (Santa Monica)—crossover at Venice and La Cienega boulevards	$380,000
57 (Orange)—northbound interchange to westbound 60	$555,000
60 (Pomona)—connector overcrossing taking eastbound 60 traffic to northbound 605	$160,000
60 (Pomona)—westbound interchange to southbound 605	$180,000
60 (Pomona)—pedestrian overcrossing near Kwis Avenue	$190,000
60 (Pomona)—pedestrian overcrossing near Riderwood Avenue	$190,000
60 (Pomona)—pedestrian overcrossing near Cogswell Road	$230,000
90 (Marina)—eastbound interchange to northbound 405	$909,000
91 (Artesia)—westbound interchange to northbound 710, across L.A. River	$870,000
134 (Ventura)—pedestrian overcrossing near Columbus Avenue	$190,000
134 (Ventura)—elevated section over L.A. River and railroad tracks	$2,140,000
134 (Ventura)—pedestrian overcrossing near Doran Street	$110,000
134 (Ventura)—westbound Orange Grove Boulevard on-ramp, overcrossing	$410,000
134 (Ventura)—eastbound interchange to northbound 2	$2,400,000
134 (Ventura)—westbound interchange to southbound 2	$720,000
134 (Ventura)—Colorado Boulevard off-ramp, overcrossing	$170,000
210 (Foothill)—pedestrian overcrossing near Broadland Avenue	$210,000
210 (Foothill)—railroad bridge crossing over the 210, near Santa Anita Avenue	$390,000
210 (Foothill)—crossover, off-ramp at Michillinda Avenue	$190,000
210 (Foothill)—westbound interchange to southbound 605	$529,000
605 (San Gabriel River)—northbound interchange to westbound 210 (Included in job above)	
405 (San Diego)—southbound connector to northbound 710	$228,000
405 (San Diego)—additional southbound connector to northbound 710 (Included in job above)	
405 (San Diego)—crossover at Exposition Boulevard and railroad tracks	$506,000
405 (San Diego)—southbound connector to westbound 10, near Exposition Boulevard (included in job above)	
405 (San Diego)—crossover at Vermont Avenue and 190th Street (Included in job above)	
10 (Santa Monica)—eastbound interchange to northbound 405	$4,029,00
405 (San Diego)—southbound interchange to eastbound 10 (Included in job above)	
405 (San Diego)—northbound interchange to westbound 10 (Included in job above)	
10 (Santa Monica)—westbound interchange to southbound 405 (Included in job above)	
405 (San Diego)—southbound interchange to eastbound 90 (Included in job above)	
605 (San Gabriel River)—crossover at railroad tracks near the Santa Fe Dam	$200,00
710 (Long Beach)—southbound interchange to eastbound 91, across L.A. River	$1,200,00
710 (Long Beach)—southbound interchange to eastbound 10	$1,526,00
5 (Golden State)—elevated section near Elysian Park (Included in job above)	

S

. Freeway Structures Declared Hazard

Occidental College

FIRE TYPE	EXTINGUISHING AGENT	METHOD
ORDINARY SOLID MATERIALS  	WATER FOAM	REMOVES HEAT REMOVES AIR AND HEAT
	DRY CHEMICAL HALON	BREAKS CHAIN REACTION
FLAMMABLE LIQUIDS  	FOAM CO_2	REMOVES AIR
	DRY CHEMICAL HALON	BREAKS CHAIN REACTION
ELECTRICAL EQUIPMENT 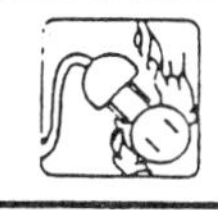 	CO_2	REMOVES AIR
	DRY CHEMICAL HALON	BREAKS CHAIN REACTION
COMBUSTIBLE METALS  	SPECIAL AGENTS	USUALLY REMOVES AIR

HOW TO USE EXTINGUISHERS

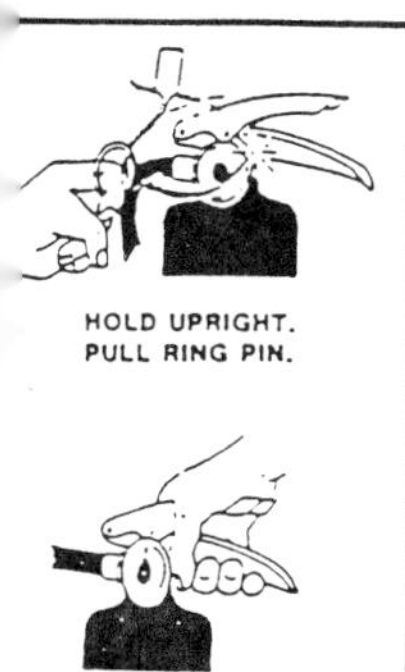

HOLD UPRIGHT.
PULL RING PIN.

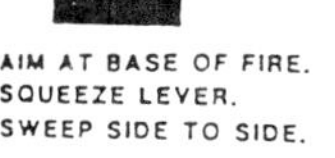

AIM AT BASE OF FIRE.
SQUEEZE LEVER.
SWEEP SIDE TO SIDE.

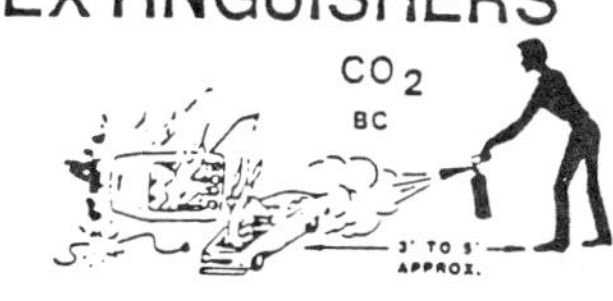

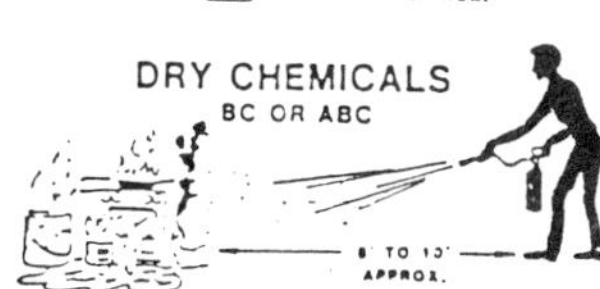

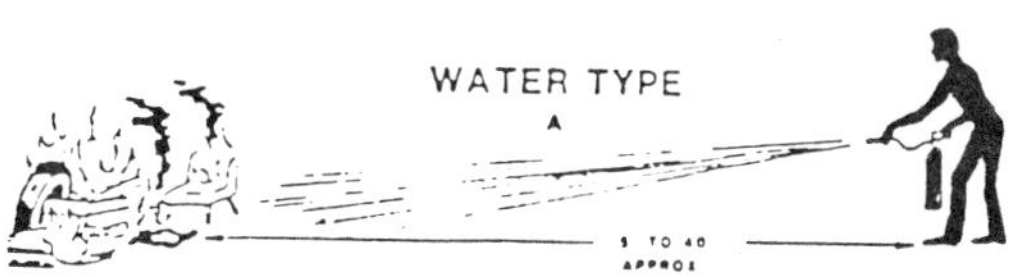

FBI BOMB DATA PROGRAM

BOMB THREAT CALL CHECKLIST

QUESTIONS TO ASK	EXACT WORDING OF THE THREAT:
1. When is bomb going to explode?	______
2. Where is it right now?	______
3. What does it look like?	______
4. What kind of bomb is it?	______
5. What will cause it to explode?	______
6. Did you place the bomb?	______
7. Why?	______
8. What is your address?	______
9. What is your name?	______

Sex of caller ______ Age ______ Race ______ Length of call ______

Figure 1 (part 1 of 2). BOMB THREAT QUESTIONNAIRE

CALLER'S VOICE:

____ Calm	____ Laughing	____ Lisp	____ Disguised
____ Angry	____ Crying	____ Raspy	____ Accent
____ Excited	____ Normal	____ Deep	____ Familiar
____ Slow	____ Distinct	____ Ragged	If voice is familiar, who did it sound like? ____
____ Rapid	____ Slurred	____ Clearing throat	
____ Soft	____ Nasal	____ Deep breathing	________
____ Loud	____ Stutter	____ Cracking voice	________

BACKGROUND SOUNDS:

____ Street noises	____ House noises	____ Factory machinery	____ Local
____ Crockery	____ Motor		____ Long distance
____ Voices	____ Office machinery	____ Animal noises	____ Booth
____ PA system		____ Clear	Other ________
____ Music		____ Static	________
			________

THREAT LANGUAGE:

____ Well spoken (educated)	____ Foul	____ Incoherent	____ Message read by threat maker
	____ Irrational	____ Taped	

REMARKS: ____

____

Report call immediately to ________________________, phone number ____________

....

Fill out completely, immediatedly after bomb threat. Date____ / __ / ____. Phone number ____________

Name ________________________. Position ____________

Figure 1 (part 2 of 2). BOMB THREAT QUESTIONNAIRE

Library Emergency Manual

Draft III, 2/11/92

Charles E. Shain Library
Greer Music Library
Connecticut College

PART A:	Summaries (Quick-reference)
PART B:	Detailed Instructions
PART C:	Resource Lists
PART D:	Appendices

PART A: SUMMARIES (quick reference)

TABLE OF CONTENTS

Connecticut College

SUMMARY OF EMERGENCY PROCEDURES FOR QUICK REFERENCE

FIRE

a. Evacuate building	Pull alarm
b. Call Campus Safety	
c. Call Library Team	

FLOODING OR WATER DAMAGE

a. Call Campus Safety	
b. Evacuate building or area if necessary	Verbal or alarm, depending on severity
c. Call Library Team	

BLACKOUT (POWER FAILURE)

a. Call Campus Safety	
b. Evacuate building	Staff member (non-student) or Campus Safety (Shain); staff in Greer
c. Shut down equipment where necessary to avoid surges	

VANDALISM/SECURITY PROBLEMS

a. Call Campus Safety

b. Call designated library supervisor (for Greer students)

PROBLEM PATRONS

Call Campus Safety
DO NOT APPROACH PERSON

Connecticut College

BOMB THREAT

a. Evacuate building — Pull fire alarm

b. Call Campus Safety

c. Contact library supervisor (Greer students)

NOTE: Order of (a) and (b) above may be reversed

*********FOR MORE COMPLETE DETAILS, SEE PART B*********

Connecticut College

PERSONS TO SUMMON WHEN A DISASTER OR EMERGENCY OCCURS

The senior staff member on duty is responsible for seeing that the emergency/disaster responses outlined on the summary pages are followed. In most cases, the staff member should also contact the Library Director and a member of the Preservation Committee (designated "Library Team" in the summary). The Preservation Committee is then responsible for contacting all other appropriate response staff as need dictates. The Committee representative must b sure to coordinate with Campus Safety.

LIBRARY DIRECTOR:

LIBRARIAN WHOSE AREA IS AFFECTED IF PROBLEM IS LOCALIZED

PRESERVATION COMMITTEE: Call in order given until you reach someone

*Should be notified of any problem in Greer

****

SECURITY (CAMPUS SAFETY):

BUILDING MANAGER (OPERATIONS):

INSURANCE/EMERGENCY FUND LIAISON:

PART B: DETAILED INSTRUCTIONS

Connecticut College

EMERGENCY EVACUATION PROCEDURES SUMMARY

The senior staff member on duty should initiate an evacuation. This will need to take place in the case of fire, bomb threat, blackout, flood, or other emergency affecting the integrity of the library building.

Evacuation may be initiated by either pulling the fire alarm or verbally alerting patrons and staff in all (or affected) library areas. The emergency procedure summary page (p.1) indicates which action is appropriate. In case of blackout, the emergency lights wil come on, but staff must have a handy supply of flashlights (with fres batteries) available.

If the emergency necessitates immediate evacuation by all persons in the building, turn over the function of checking for anyone remaining in the building to the appropriate authorities.

The library staff (regular and student) should plan to gather at the designated meeting spot following evacuation for attendance.

Shain staff:	Lawn in front of main entrance
Greer staff:	Lawn in center of Castle Court

FIRE

1. Fire alarms are located at each exit and at other locations throughout Shain and Cummings Arts Center (See Map in Appendix VI).

2. Follow the instructions for emergency evacuation procedures (p.B1).

INFORMATION FOR DEALING WITH FIRE EMERGENCIES:

1. When an alarm is activated, an alarm is sounded within the library and Campus Safety is notified automatically. They will call the New London Fire Department.

2. Leave the building in an orderly fashion, preferably by the MAIN EXIT which can open to four doors to accommodate many people (same for Greer). Staff in technical services may want to use the exit to the loading dock. A-V staff should use the nearest emergency exit on the lower level. Use any of the emergency exits if necessary. Greer staff and patrons should proceed out the nearest unblocked exit, preferably to the courtyard or to the loading dock.

CAMPUS SAFETY OR THE FIRE DEPARTMENT WILL CHECK EACH FLOOR TO MAKE SURE THAT THE BUILDING HAS BEEN EVACUATED COMPLETELY.

3. When the fire alarm goes off, the elevator automatically returns to the main floor and the doors open. From this point, it can no longer be used (not applicable to Greer).

4. In case of a power failure, the emergency generator goes on within thirty seconds, providing enough light so that people can exit the building safely.

OTHER INFORMATION:

1. There are smoke and heat detectors in the machinery room. There is one heat detector in the kitchen of the Staff Room, which automatically triggers the fire alarm when the temperature reaches 135 degrees. (Shain)

2. Neither Shain nor Greer has a sprinkler system.

3. There are 5 water-type fire extinguishers on each of the main floors, with one in each stairwell behind a glass door. There are at least 5 on the lower level, a mixture of the water and chemical types. Extinguishers are regularly checked by the campus fire warden. The extinguishers are meant to be used in a fire emergency if necessary but since they are heavy and unwieldy, it would be best to leave their use to trained fire fighters. (Shain)

Greer has a fire extinguisher located next to the public NOTIS terminals.

4. The metal doors in each stairwell have a 2-hour fire rating. When the fire alarm sounds, vents in the roof at the top of each stairwell open automatically to vent smoke from the stairwell.

5. In the landings on the stairwell, and in the corridor outside Greer, there are folded-up water hoses. These are connected to a "standpipe system" to be used by TRAINED FIRE FIGHTERS ONLY.

Connecticut College

FLOOD EMERGENCY

1. Follow the evacuation/notification procedures found in the emergency procedures summary section. (p. B1)

2. Make certain that all staff/patrons keep away from flooded areas until the proper authorities determine that the danger of electrocution is ended.

3. Once the area is safe to enter, implement damage control measures to minimize water damage to library materials and equipment. See Appendix III for instructions on dealing with water-damaged materials.

DAMAGE CONTROL:

-- Notify the power house to maintain the temperature at 50-60 degrees. Bring in dehumidifiers to dry the air.

-- Keep the air circulating. Open doors and windows if possible. Install fans.

-- Contact the NEDCC (24-hour disaster coverage).

-- Begin damage assessment.

DAMAGE ASSESSMENT:

-- Identify the types of materials damaged and the extent of the damage.

-- Determine the nature of the damage (damp or wet; oily, muddy, or clear water).

-- Determine if other damage has also occurred (fire, soot, heat).

-- Photograph the area before any salvage work begins.

RECLAMATION:

-- Organize a command center.

-- Assess equipment needs (fans, generators, dehumidifiers, sump pumps, freezer trucks, etc.)

-- Arrange for inspection by the insurance carrier.

-- Check on emergency fund availability.

-- Begin salvaging materials (see Appendix III for instructions).

All of the above must be done within 48-72 hours. Mold growth on wet materials will take hold after this time.

Connecticut College

COMPUTER SYSTEMS EMERGENCY PROCEDURES

CTW problems

Computer system failure is defined here as an event which prevents or threatens the normal operation of the computer system as a whole, not problems with individual terminals or printers.

During the day, contact one of the following people:

During evenings and weekends, if trouble shooting fails:

Trouble shooting:

1. Try to "unlock" an individual terminal.
2. Check the printer to which the non-functioning terminal is attached.
3. Call Alan or Bu at home only when the whole system is down, or if all of the public or tech. serv. terminals are down.
4. If all terminals in the system are not responding, press the RESET button on the Terminal Server in Tech. Services.

Put an "out of order" sign on individual terminals or the "system down" sign (kept in Jeanette's office) on the OPAC cluster in the lobby.

At Greer Music Library:

The Greer student assistant on duty evenings and weekends should call the Shain Circulation and/or Reference Desk for information and guidance should the NOTIS system fail.

InfoTrac problems:

During the day: Call a member of the Reference Dept. staff.

During evenings and weekends, try the following steps:

1. Check the printer. Turn it off if necessary to make InfoTrac function. The printer and the computer are separate machines. Do not try to print if printer is turned off.

2. Turn off InfoTrac (press "power" at lower right) and reboot. Follow menu prompts.

*Primary contact person

3. Place "out of order" sign on machine with date and your initials. Refer patrons to DWIL or to printed indexes.

4. The InfoTrac manual is kept on bookshelf behind Ref. Desk.

CD-ROM problems:

During the day, contact one of the following people:

During evenings and weekends, try the following:

1. Press <F10> Q.
2. Press <CTRL><ALT><DEL> to reboot.
3. If a set of function keys shows up on screen with arrow pointer, press that function key. The problem may clear.
4. It is okay to turn an individual terminal on and off.
5. If only one terminal and/or printer is not working, put an "out of order" sign on it.
6. Consult the "activity log" (blue notebook on shelf above CD-ROM server) for more suggestions.
7. If the whole CD-ROM network has stopped functioning, Tim Groome may be contacted on his beeper ((when prompted).
8. Put up a sign indicating that the CD-ROM network is not working. Patrons may be directed to the printed indexes, DWIL, and InfoTrac.

OCLC problems:

During the day:

OCLC User Contact Desk 9-1-800-848-5800

Evening and weekends: OCLC is only available at night until 10 p.m. and is not available on Sunday. Call User Contact Desk on Saturday.

Power failures:

A power failure is the most common emergency for the computer systems. The PCs and OCLC terminals are connected to surge protectors but if the power fails and is off for more than a few minutes, the computers should be turned off and unplugged from electrical outlets wherever possible. After the power supply is reestablished, the machines may be plugged in and turned on again.

If we know in advance of a planned or probable electrical failure (e.g. hurricane), disconnect all machines. Call Alan Hagyard or Tim Groome ( ).

*Primary contact person

Connecticut College

COLLAPSE OF SHELVING AND OTHER STRUCTURAL ACCIDENTS

Anyone noticing a minor collapse or structural accident with no injuries should contact a staff member as soon as possible, indicating the location of the problem. Staff should notify the senior staff member on duty. He/she should make an assessment of the situation and determine what action is warranted. The department head should be informed of the problem.

In the case of major shelving collapse or structural accident with injuries, the staff should call Campus Safety. If a patron is trapped, tell Campus Safety to call the Fire Department and an ambulance. Do not attempt to move the injured patron. Do not panic. The unsafe area should be cleared of patrons.

Campus Safety

See Floor Plans, Appendix VI.

VANDALISM/SECURITY PROBLEMS

1. For a serious act of vandalism or security problem, contact Campus Safety from an office phone. Remain calm. Do not confront the perpetrator.

2. Minor vandalism: Staff should be alerted as soon as possible.

3. If the gate security system goes off, ask the patron to please come back through the gate, and alert the staff member on duty. In cases of suspected theft, the staff member should get the name of the violator and fill out a security violation form. A copy of this form goes to the Director of the Library and the Head of Circulation. One of these people will contact either Campus Safety or the "J-Board" chairman. If the violator is a Connecticut College student, the "J-Board" will determine what disciplinary action will take place.

Connecticut College

PROBLEM PATRONS

1. Problem patrons may be Connecticut College students, staff, or faculty or they may be a member of the outside community. A problem patron is any person who is behaving in an unacceptable manner. This individual may be overly rambunctious and disagreeable or quiet and discomforting. If the individual is annoying another patron or a staff member in any way, the person is a problem patron.

2. Remain calm. Try not to overreact. Do not approach the problem patron. Never follow or run after a problem patron.

3. Call Security. If possible use an office phone, not a desk phone It is best to call as little attention as possible to the situation and to the individual in question.

CAMPUS SAFETY

BOMB THREATS

Follow the instructions given in the emergency procedures summary section. (p. B1). Please note the following:

1. If a suspicious object or package is found, Campus Safety should be notified at once.

2. If a staff member receives a call reporting a bomb threat, he or she should remain calm and try to secure answers to the following questions:

   a. When will the bomb explode?
   b. Where is the bomb?
   c. When was it planted?
   d. What does the bomb look like?
   e. What type of bomb is it?

3. The staff member receiving the threat should carefully note the following:

   a. The EXACT words used by the caller.
   b. Explicit motive for the threat.
   c. Quality of voice. Does the caller sound young or old, male or female? Does the caller have an accent: Does he or she sound nervous, determined, etc.?
   d. Any background noise.

Campus Safety recommends calling its office before evacuating a building. The staff member receiving the threat may initiate evacuation, however, if the nature of the call and attitude of the caller seems to warrant immediate action. Err on the side of safety.

NATURAL DISASTERS

A natural disaster may leave water damage, electrical failure, and/or structural degradation of buildings in its wake. Consult the appropriate sections of this manual for instructions on dealing with these problems. Coordination between Preservation Committee members and campus authorities will be crucial in handling any or all of the after effects of a natural disaster.

While most natural disasters can happen with little or no warning (tornados, earthquakes), the library can prepare for certain events:

1. Should local civil defense and weather reports indicate that a hurricane will affect the area, the library should take the following precautions:

    -- Tape windows

    -- Unplug electrical equipment and remove wires from floor

    -- Cover equipment and library materials with plastic sheets in areas known to suffer from water problems during storms

    -- Remove valuable equipment and materials from floors

2. Keep in close contact with Campus Safety. The library should have a radio on hand in order to listen to reports.

In the case of hurricanes, the library will most likely be shut down before the storm arrives in the area. Campus Safety should be responsible for notifying the Library Director in the case of storm damage. The Library Director can then contact a member of the Preservation Committee. Campus Safety should also be asked to check both libraries periodically during (or immediately following) a stor

Tornados and earthquakes can strike without warning, although storm warnings may be posted that would forewarn of the possibility of a tornado. If a tornado warning siren sounds, staff should direct patrons to the lower levels of the building (Shain and Cummings) as quickly as possible. Stay away from windows.

If an earthquake strikes, evacuate immediately. Desks and heavy tables and doorways can offer some protection. Following the shock library staff should gather at the evacuation meeting area for attendance. DO NOT REENTER THE BUILDING.

NUCLEAR ACCIDENTS

If the sirens sound an alarm, listen to either the loudspeakers (mounted on the poles, but difficult to understand) or the radio to find out what is happening. In the case of a nuclear event requiring immediate evacuation, library staff should follow the evacuation plan developed by the city and Campus Safety (in process). Please note that the telephone book contains a map showing which routes residents should take to leave the area.

Bruce Ayers is in charge of all emergency evacuation plans.

Connecticut College

GAS LEAKS/CHEMICAL EMERGENCIES

Most applicable to Greer Music Library (gas lines in Cummings and chemicals used in art classes):

1. If you smell gas, evacuate the library. Other departments must be responsible for their own areas in Cummings. The gas utilities recommend calling the proper authorities from a telephone outside the building, as electrical sparks could cause an explosion.

2. Follow the procedures for evacuation. (p. B1)

3. Do not reenter the building until the proper authorities have indicated that it is safe to do so.

4. Since the chemical added to the gas to create a noticeable odor is quite strong and can make some people ill, and it takes time for the ventilation system to replace the "dirty" air with fresh, the librarian should use judgement as to whether the library should be reopened immediately once the building is declared safe.

FOR OTHER CHEMICAL FUMES:

1. Call Campus Safety. Unless the situation seems critical (i.e., people are becoming ill or some other factor seems to indicate immediate danger), the staff member on duty may opt to delay evacuating the library until he/she has had the opportunity to consult with the proper authorities.

2. Follow the procedures for evacuation.

MOLD

Mold can occur whenever temperature and humidity climb above 55 degrees Fahrenheit and 50% relative humidity (plus/minus 5%) and mold spores are present. Once a mold infestation takes hold, it is very difficult to control and can re-occur again and again when conditions are right.

1. If the infestation is limited to a few items, isolate those items. These can be cleaned by hand using one of the techniques recommended by the NEDCC (see Appendix II).

2. If the infestation is widespread, take immediate action to stabilize the collection.

   -- Control the temperature and humidity (install dehumidifiers) to the recommended limits

   -- Improve air circulation

Large-scale infestation will mean coordinating cleaning efforts with Physical Plant. The Library Director should be notified of mold problems, and the designated staff member should work closely with Physical Plant staff when the clean-up begins.

AN INFESTED AREA SHOULD BE DEHUMIDIFIED AS QUICKLY AS POSSIBLE.

Connecticut College

RODENTS AND INSECTS

1. When standards of temperature, humidity and cleanliness are less than ideal, the collection may be subject to damage from insect and rodent infestation. Insects such as cockroaches and silverfish will eat paper. Rodents can also destroy library materials.

2. If evidence of infestation is found, the staff should notify the Library Director. Either he or his designated representative will contact Physical Plant concerning the problem.

3. Attempt to isolate infested material from the rest of the collection. Identify the type and extent of the infestation.

FUMIGATION

Should the College decide to exterminate or fumigate, make certain that the chemicals used meet the following RLG criteria:*

Fumigants should:

- -- Be rapid and powerful
- -- Have no residual toxicity for humans
- -- Have no adverse effects on the constituent elements c the material being treated (check with NEDCC)
- -- Be applied by a properly trained professional

*from RLG PRESERVATION MANUAL

Connecticut College

PART C

RESOURCE LISTS

RECOVERY RESOURCES

(The following list was derived from recommendations by the State of Connecticut, NEDCC, and The American Antiquarian Society)

American Freeze-Dry, Inc.
vacuum freeze drying
411 White Horse Pike, Audubon, NJ 08106 1-609-546-0777

Blackburn Janitorial
mold clean-up; water, fire damage
1495 Hartford Tpke., Oakdale, CT 06370 1-203-443-5007

Ernest A. Conrad, P.E.
consultant; highly recommended by NEDCC
President, Landmark Facilities Group, Inc.
252 East Avenue, Norwalk, CT 06855 1-203-866-4626

Library of Congress Preservation Office
consulting services 1-202-287-5213

McDonnell Aircraft Co.
freeze-drying
Box 516, St. Louis, MO 63166 1-314-232-0232

Moisture Control Services (Cargocaire)
24-hour service; fire and water damage;
recommended highly by NEDCC
20 Del Carmine Street, Wakefield, MA 01880 1-617-245-6021

Northeast Document Conservation Center (NEDCC)
maintains 24-hour emergency service line 1-800-470-1010

ADDITIONAL IN-HOUSE RESOURCES (PEOPLE TO CALL):

Manager of Maintenance; Environmental

Supervisor, Custodial Services

Manager/Material Control

FREEZER TRUCKS

(See Appendix III for complete instructions.)

Please note:

All firms require drivers to hold a Class II license.

A. Edart

a. 739-3423

b. Summer months - may not have many or any trucks immediately available, but can guide us to other firms that have trucks

c. Seems willing to accommodate emergency situation - does not require previous credit application from Connecticut College

d. Connecticut College must pay insurance on the rental truck(s)

B. Ryder

a. 1-800-888-0425

b. Requires establishment of credit first (i.e., must have an approved form on file)

c. Seems sure that would be able to get us a truck within the 48-72 hour window

C. Budget Car and Truck Rental

a. 447-0374

b. Trucks available, but in Rhode Island -- uncertain whether firm would drive them to Connecticut for us (if not, our driver(s) would have to go to Rhode Island)

EMERGENCY FUNDING AND INSURANCE

CONTACT:

Office of the <u>Controller</u> for emergency funding (. The College has a bank card which can be used for this purpose. Campus Safety will contact an office representative during off hours.

Office of the <u>Vice President for Finance</u> for insurance claims (,. The College's insurance is handled by Allen, Russell and Alle in Hartford ( ). We are advised to take whatever steps may be necessary to avoid further damage before the adjustor can reach campus. Take as many photographs as possible.

PART D: APPENDICES

I Inventory of Supplies on Hand

II Basic Directions for Dealing with Moldy Materials

III Basic Directions for Dealing with Water-damaged Materials

IV Basic Directions for Dealing with Fire-damaged Materials

V Basic Directions for Salvaging Non-print Materials

VI Floor Plans of Shain and Greer

Connecticut College

APPENDIX I
INVENTORY OF SUPPLIES

EMERGENCY SUPPLY BOXES: /MILK CRATES OR COVERED PLASTIC BINS/

Flashlights/batteries (batteries will be replaced each year during the annual review of the Emergency Manual)
Duct Tape
Extension cords
Freezer paper
Paper towels (plain white; 2 rolls)
Plastic garbage bags (Hefty steel sack; several)
Plastic sheeting (folded)
Toothpicks (rounded ends only; 1 box)
String (1 ball)
Marker (permanent)
Masking tape
Rubber gloves (medium, 2 pr.)
Sponges (heavy-duty, large; 2)
Scissors
Notebook/pen or pencil

OTHER:

Clean newsprint (keep in safe, dry area to have on hand)
Lint-free cloths
Hair dryers with "air" setting
Book trucks (from Circulation)
Shain camera (lower drawer, Jeanette's desk)
Fans
Brooms (custodial)
Buckets (custodial)
Cardboard cartons (request from College when needed - for packing)
Ladders (custodial)
Mops (custodial)
Water vacuums (custodial)

APPENDIX II
DEALING WITH MOLD

The presence of mold indicates a problem with the amount of moisture (relative humidity) in the air. Levels over the ideal of 50% (+-5%) can set the stage for mold infestation.

If only a small number of items are affected, the staff can try to isolate these materials and clean them using an appropriate method. In some cases the mold can be wiped off with a clean cloth. NEDCC does not recommend the use of chemicals such as thymol and o-phenyl phenol, which are highly toxic. While ethanol alcohol can be used for a very small number of items, the substance can damage a book unless spot-tested first and used under careful supervision.

NEDCC recommends vacuuming as the best way of dealing with most mold infestations.

a. Use triple-filter vacuums.
b. Wipe down shelves and walls/floors with an approved agent (preferably one with no water).
c. Always wear masks and other protective clothing.

The single most important factor in bringing the collection to recovery is to lower the humidity as soon as possible. The mold will be more difficult to remove if the air is still wet. If the humidity is not controlled, mold will return in the future, worse than before. The spores are always present in the air. Air circulation should be increased in the affected area as well.

If materials suffer water damage, steps must be taken within 48-72 hours to dry or freeze the items before mold growth begins.

APPENDIX III
DEALING WITH WATER-DAMAGED MATERIALS

Reduce the humidity level in the affected area as quickly as possible and increase air circulation. Reduce the temperature.

Handle damaged materials as little as possible.

MANUAL DRYING:

If a very small number of items is affected, manual drying may be attempted.

1. Set up tables in a secure, dry area (or outside if the air is dry).
2. Cover the tables with clean newsprint (paper towels also acceptable).
3. Interleave the pages of the books with clean newsprint.
4. Set the books up on the table for drying.

FREEZING/THAWING:

The best method of salvaging wet items is through freezing. A freez truck should be hired from one of the firms listed on page C2.

1. Open the books, as above, and interleave with clean newsprint (this helps absorb moisture).
2. Pack (1 layer only!) into cardboard boxes, curving a piece of wax paper (freezer paper acceptable) over the book (U-shape)*. Place each book spine-down in the box.
3. Try to maintain low temperature/low humidity levels during the transfer of materials to the freezer facility.
4. Keep careful inventory records of what is being shipped.

*You do not actually wrap each book tightly, as in a package.

Following freezing:

Once the wet books are frozen, the Preservation Team can plan the ne course of action. The Team must decide where to send the books and how to do so. Unless one of the mass freezer firms sends out its ow transports, we would probably have to hire a commercial trucking fir to bring the books to the company.

Special and non-print formats may require special care. The Preservation Committee should work closely with experts/conservators to determine the best course of action.

THAWING:

Before thawing occurs, the Preservation Committee should consult a conservator to ascertain the next steps. Some materials may need additional cleaning if they have been exposed to mud, oil, or other substances.

APPENDIX IV
DEALING WITH FIRE-DAMAGED MATERIALS

Determine which items are salvageable. The Library should have a plan in place to deal with unsalvageable materials. Photocopying some damaged items might be an option.

The Preservation Committee should consult an expert/conservator experienced in handling fire-damaged materials.

APPENDIX V
SALVAGING NON-PRINT MATERIALS

Should non-print materials such as films and tapes become water-damaged, the Library Team should probably consult a conservator exper in the field. In general, however, films, tapes and photographs should be loosened from their containers in order to prevent layers from sticking together. Sound recordings must be removed from jacket and carefully wiped dry.

Software

An article appeared in the November 1986 issue of College and Researc Libraries News (p. 634) explaining how the library at Mankato State University salvaged wet floppy disks. The following is an extract taken from Nancy Olson's article outlining the basic steps of salvaging software:

1. For disks not thoroughly soaked (no water spurts out when squeezed):

   Set hair dryer on "air" setting (NOT heat).

   Hold disk sleeve slightly away from disk, and direct air into the sleeve, drying all sides of sleeve and disk, and all corners.

   Once dry, make copy of the disk.

2. For dripping wet disks:

   Peel out of plastic sleeves. If a paper cutter is necessary for stubborn sleeves, be sure to tap the disk away from the edge being cut.

   Wipe each disk dry with a soft, lint-free cloth.

   Hang the disk for further drying.

   To copy dried disks:
   - Cut open a new dry disk by trimming about 1/16 inch of the write-protect edge with a paper cutter.
   - Remove disk and set aside for later replacement.
   - Slip the dried disks one by one into this temporary she and copy.